Ghost Railways of
Ontario
Volume 2

This Book is the Property of

Michael Jack

Happy 30th Birthday!
Pat & Jon.

Ron Brown

Polar Bear Press, Toronto

distributed by:
North 49 Books
35 Prince Andrew Place
Toronto, Ontario M3C 2H2
416 449-4000
north49@idirect.com

Canadian Cataloguing in Publication Data

Brown, Ron, 1945-
 Ghost railways of Ontario: volume 2

1st ed.
includes bibliographical references and index.
ISBN 1-896757-14-6

1. Railroads – Ontario – Guidebooks   2. Ontario – Guidebooks.   I. Title

HE2809.05B76 2000   385.09713   C00-930455-X

Printed in Canada

2000 01 01 02   10 9 8 7 6 5 4 3 2 1

Table of Contents

Eastern Ontario

Cottage Country

Northern Ontario

Introduction

As with *Ghost Railways of Ontario: Volume One*, this book leads you to, and along, Ontario's many abandoned railway corridors. Abandonments are no new thing. They have been occurring for over a century. The Cobourg and Peterborough Railway was shut down north of Rice Lake after just seven years of operation when the ice flow in the lake proved too much for its fragile trestle. The Grand Trunk abandoned much of its shoreline section between Port Hope and Oshawa when waves washed the roadbed into the lake.

Railway companies have long stood accused of manipulating their way out of local freight and passenger service. While local service may have been less economical than long distance hauling, they were seldom *un*economical. The success of short lines on these so-called uneconomical lines have proven that. What drives up the cost of train travel is the unreasonable rates charged by track owners, such as CN and CP, for the passage of passenger trains over their lines. One source assured this writer that the cost which CN charges the ONR for its Northlander to run on CN tracks between North Bay and Toronto is so exorbitant that the Northlander cannot break even when running full. Yet the actual costs to those track owners for light weight passenger trains is negligible, particularly when compared to the long and heavy freight trains which are far more numerous. In short, the railway giants simply don't want passenger trains using their tracks.

For its failure to remedy this abuse, society is already paying the price. Road repairs are consuming ever larger chunks of the public purse. The proliferation of truck traffic is worsening pollution, and increasing driving hazards, while auto-oriented land use consumes valuable farm land, as it lowers the quality of life.

Where does the blame lie? Clearly the federal government must assume responsibility for deregulating the railways and for abandoning Canada's rail passenger service. Reform-style provincial governments, such as those in Ontario and Alberta, philosophically place private profit above the public good by abandoning land use controls, and stripping public transit of most of its funding. Many local governments likewise ignore the need for public transit on the assumption that such service might encourage lower income families to move in and tarnish their municipal paradises.

And so the ghost railways increase.

This volume documents a further 26 such routes, in addition to those featured in the first volume. The lines in the present volume were either not included in the first book, or have been abandoned in the interim. Further, this volume includes several electric interurban railways, a form of railway omitted from the first volume. (Most of Ontario's larger communities possessed at least one. Hamilton had four).

Despite the folly of abandoning the trackage in the first place, the development of trails is an encouraging sign. Several routes in this book are not just rail trails, but are incorporated into the Trans Canada Trail network. The objective of this national corridor is to develop a continuous trail from coast to coast which permits a variety of trail activities, although it discourages motorized use where possible. But it does not forbid it. In many regions of Canada, the use of snowmobiles is more than just a form of recreation, it is often a major means of travel, and the rail trails are the ideal avenues for them. Indeed, many rail trails would not exist at all were it not for the initiative of and maintenance by snowmobile clubs.

In other cases, where municipalities have lacked the political will, and adjacent land owners lacked the public interest, the routes are no more. Still, the old station locations can be identified, while the villages that grew around them often retain businesses or buildings that began with the arrival of the trains.

Celebrating our railway heritage involves more than just driving around and snapping photos. There will be little left to photograph if we do not make our concerns about this disappearing heritage known to our decision makers. Let your local town councillor, your MPP or your MP know you care.

How to Use This Book

Ontario's railway heritage has mostly been forgotten, and is all too often ignored. This book hopes to help change that.

This volume helps the heritage follower to chase these old lines regardless of their condition or their re-use. Even where rail trails exist the directions are geared toward the car driver, for even the trail user relies on the auto to reach the start of the trail. Many of the abandoned lines have passed out of public ownership, roads remain the only means to follow them. Where the rail corridors have become trails, directions to trail users are not as critical. The trails are self-evident, and are usually accompanied with trail guide literature.

While much of the description in this book deals with the vestiges of the railways themselves, an equal amount is directed towards the landscapes which evolved or changed because of them. Hotels, feed mills, and even entire communities appeared with the arrival of the railways. These, too, are as much a part of Ontario's railway heritage as are the stations and the bridges.

Sadly, it is not easy to find physical evidence of that heritage. Few municipalities seem interested in celebrating the very features which brought them their prosperity, or in some cases, their very existence. This book points out those surviving features.

While directions are included in each chapter, the user of this book may wish to consult a map. The most comprehensive maps available for the southern portion of the province are found in MapArt Publishing's "Ontario Road Atlas". Unlike the MTO maps, this atlas gives not just the road numbers, but their names as well. And it has up-to-date information on the vast number of changes to Ontario's road numbers which followed the Ontario government's controversial transfer of provincial highways to local municipalities.

For more detail the user should also refer to the federal 1:50,000 scale topographic maps. These show every feature of the landscape, including rail lines, bridges and buildings, as well as vegetation and land contours. Unlike the MapArt atlas, these maps are not widely available. For example, Ontario's Ministry of Natural Resources no longer sells them. A complete collection, however, is available in Toronto's main reference library on Yonge St but they are not current.

For northern Ontario, the user should refer to MNR's one inch to one mile series of maps. While lacking the topographic detail of the 1:50,000 series, they do show roads, rail lines, water bodies, and a limited number of buildings.

The lengths of the routes in this volume vary quite markedly. Some routes, such as the St Mary's and Western, can be covered in a couple of hours. Others, like the Canadian Northern's Algonquin route, may require two or three days.

You should also anticipate the nature of the ownership of the rights of way. Where corridors have not yet been disposed of by the railway companies, they remain the private property of those companies, and may be posted. Many of the buildings that relate to these routes are also private. While you may photograph them freely from any public vantage point, permission is required if you wish to take a picture while on private property.

Ontario's railway heritage is still there to be seen, and *Ghost Railways of Ontario: Volume Two* shows the way.

Ron Brown
March, 2000

1.

The Lost Electrics of Southwestern Ontario

They came by the thousands during those late summer days in 1884. What they waited to see was North America's first electric streetcar. Here, at the Toronto Agricultural Fair, the precursor to today's Canadian National Exhibition (or "The Ex" to its legions of fans,) they gasped as an electrically powered engine rattled along a set of tracks with three open passenger cars in tow, each jammed with awe-struck adventurers. Following an age of stage coaches and steam locomotives, the electric street railway was a phenomenon. And it would revolutionize transportation around the world.

For the first summer of its exhibition, power came through a copper strip embedded in the track. But the following year, the more familiar overhead wires put in their appearance. Because the railways could not provide local neighbourhood service, and because horse drawn stage coaches were jolting and slow, the electric street railway craze spread quickly. By 1900 Ontario had 205 km (128 miles) of line, by 1910, 553.

While those emanating out of Toronto could claim 219 km (137 miles) of track, Hamilton had the most lines with four, although their combined trackage totaled only 125 km (78 miles). The Grand River area could claim 142 km (89 miles), the Niagara area 118 km (74 miles), while southwestern Ontario boasted the second most extensive network with 150 km (94 miles) of electric railway trackage.

More than 87 electric railways were proposed across Ontario. Most, however, were never built. One of the most enthusiastic proponents was not a commercial operator, but rather the first chairman of the Ontario Hydro Electric Power Commission, later Ontario Hydro, Adam Beck. With a massive source of electric power at his disposal, he proposed railway networks which would link Toronto with Sarnia, Port

Perry and Fort Erie. Indeed, were it not for two small gaps in Ontario's radial railway network, one of 17½ km (11 miles) west of Port Credit, and another of 11 km (7 miles) between Vineland and St Catharines, this province would have had a radial railway network which would have extended from Toronto and Guelph into New York state, and from there to the entire U.S. Midwest.

But by the 1920s the auto age was arriving. Car, gasoline and tire manufacturers were aggressively lobbying for the cessation of electric street railways and their replacement with buses. In the U.S. a consortium of such businesses was convicted of conspiring to acquire and close down the streetcar service in a large number of mid-sized American towns. Whether such shenanigans occurred in Ontario has never been proven.

More winds of change occurred with the election of the anti-railway government of E.C. Drury in 1923. When he refused loan guarantees to the municipalities which would build them, Beck's dreams of a province wide radial railway network died.

Electric railways dwindled from nearly 1280 km (800 miles) at their peak in 1920 to less than half of that two decades later. When the last radial coach clanged into its terminal for the last time in 1959, 387 km (242 miles) of electric miles still operated, but all was devoted to freight.

There is often confusion over terms like "radial," "interurban," and "electric" railway. Generally, electric street railways were streetcar lines which provided street passenger service within a single municipality. Radials, the Canadian term, or interurbans, the American equivalent, operated *between* cities, and often carried freight to the steam railways.

Theirs is a legacy which has largely vanished from the landscape and from memory as well. They were less glamorous than steam, and by running on or beside roads which later were widened or paved, they have left little to see on the landscape. Most of their stations were small shelters, or consisted of waiting rooms in the front portion of office buildings. Few single purpose radial stations were built, fewer have survived.

While many ghost railways live on in lore and legend, the electrics remain largely forgotten. Were it not for the determined efforts of a few local historians, southwestern Ontario's long gone radial railways would remain relegated to dusty statute books.

The Windsor Essex and Lakeshore Rapid Railway: Windsor to Leamington

Known as the "Sunshine County Route," the purpose of this line across Essex County was to tap into the booming rural growth here in southwestern Ontario's most populous county. Although incorporated as early as 1879, its charter was not acted upon until 1901. Its provisions envisioned extensions as far as Wheatley and Tilbury.

During construction, the WELR came up against the Michigan Central which stubbornly refused the electric line permission to cross its own main line in Essex, a standoff eventually resolved by the Board of Railway Commissioners, the federal government's railway watchdog.

Finally, in September of 1907 the electric cars began rattling between Windsor and Essex. Shortly after that they began rolling into Kingsville and then in April 1908 into Leamington. This, however, was as far as they got. The extensions to Wheatley and Tilbury remained paper dreams only. In 1919 the Hydro Electric Power Commission of Ontario Hydro, became involved with the operation of electric railways across Ontario, and took over the WELR.

The WELR carried a small amount of freight, mainly from the canning factories near Leamington, connecting with the CPR, the Michigan Central, the Essex Terminal and the Pere Marquette Railways. After operating quite profitably for a number of years, the WELR reached its peak with one million passengers in 1921. But the inevitable bus competition appeared in the 1920s, and, to compete, the WELR began operating a couple of buses of its own. Still, by 1928, passenger traffic had fallen by two-thirds.

In 1928 the HEPC did the unthinkable. Flaunting the looming auto age, and falling profits, HEPC began to upgrade the line. They replaced trackage, upgraded the electric infrastructure, and placed orders for new cars. In 1930 they began to make plans for a new Windsor terminal on land which it optioned at Sandwich, Ferry and Pitt Streets. The new terminal would serve both the electric lines and the fledgling bus lines. But it would never be built.

The new cars were indeed the latest in luxury. With the words "Sunshine County Route" boldly emblazoned on the side, they contained smoking compartments with leather settees, a main compartment with 28 upholstered seats and a 15-foot solarium at each end of the car. And they were heated, electrically.

But all the new equipment in the world could not compete with the auto age, especially when the depression hit. By 1930 the WELR was losing $150,000 a year, an amount unacceptable to the many little municipalities along the line. In September of 1932 the line was shut down, and within three years the tracks had been removed.

 **All Aboard** --

The route ran from a store-front waiting room at Pitt and Ouelette St in downtown Windsor. It then followed Pitt to Mercator Pl, Chatham St E., and Aylmer Ave before heading south on Howard Ave. It then followed Highway 3 along the north side to Maidstone where it switched to the south side of the road. At Cottam it swung south to enter Kingsville on Division St, and a small waiting room and office a short distance east on Main St. While the main line followed Main St east through Kingsville, a branch line went south on Lansdowne to Lakeside Park where it accessed the lake, the shops and the powerhouse.

From the southern outskirts of Ruthven, it followed a private right of way, which is still visible. Entering Leamington on Oak St, one branch swung north up Erie St to Highway 3, while another branch swung south to carry excursionists to the lake shore at Seacliffe Park.

Road widening and paving has removed most traces of the WELR. The only vestige is the overgrown private alignment west of Leamington. Here and there buildings which were tied to the railway have survived, such as a pair of lakeside hotels on Park St in Kingsville. For the most part though, the old WELR is another railway heritage lost.

The Sandwich Windsor and Amherstburg Railway

The first section was built between Windsor and Walkerville in 1886 and became Canada's first regular electric streetcar line. In 1891 it was reorganized as the Sandwich Windsor and Amherstburg Railway and in 1901 passed into the hands of Detroit United, then operating the electrical systems across the border.

From downtown Windsor the route followed city streets to the Detroit River near Sunnyside where it swung inland to avoid a marshy area. It then returned to its river route which it followed into

Amherstburg.

The Tecumseh portion of the line paralleled the river through Walkerville to Tecumseh, then a suburb of Windsor.

The franchise expired in 1919 and was purchased by the municipalities through which it passed, and was contracted out to HEPC. Hydro upgraded the line in 1924-25 to allow it to carry freight, a fairly common practice among eclectic railway lines. By the 1930s buses began to carry more passengers than the railways, and in 1934, HEPC cancelled its contract with the municipalities. Unable to operate the line on their own, the local politicians closed it down in 1937. Today, urban sprawl has so completely engulfed the area through which it ran that nothing remains of it to be seen.

The Woodstock, Thames Valley and Ingersoll Railway

Perhaps one of Ontario's shortest radial railways was the Woodstock, Thames Valley and Ingersoll Railway. Its main promoters were a pair of out-of-towners named J. Armstrong and S. Ritter Ickes who dreamed of a much wider network of radial lines which would link Woodstock with Niagara Falls, Windsor and Toronto.

In 1901 it began operating between Woodstock and Ingersoll using a tiny "Tooterville Trolley" style 24-seater nicknamed Estelle. (The real Estelle, it was later revealed, was Ickes' daughter.)

Along with the City of Woodstock, Estelle operated from a waiting room in the McLeod Building at Dundas St. and Broadway, before following Mill, Huron and Park Row to present-day CR 9. Like many other interurbans it created a park to attract more customers, Fairmount Park on the Thames River east of Beachville. Here campers and excursionists filled the little coach to capacity. Winters were not so pleasant, as the heater in the car failed to cast consistent heat, being either too hot, too smokey or not hot enough. Its western terminus was the Ingersoll Inn.

The 18 km (11 ½ mile) line operated from 1902 to 1925 before being replaced with buses. Road paving and widening have removed all traces of this little lost line.

The Chatham Wallaceburg and Lake Erie Railway: Wallaceburg to Erie Beach

The longest and most durable of the lost electric lines of south-

Small bridge abutments are occasionally visible beside Baldoon Road, the route of CWL north of Chatham.

western Ontario was the Chatham Wallaceburg and Lake Erie Railway.

The line was first chartered in 1903 at the instigation of the business communities in Wallaceburg and Chatham. But as was often the case, funds were hard to find. Then, in 1905, with money raised from a surprising source, a group in Towanda Pennsylvania, construction began in Wallaceburg. It reached Chatham, however, before Chatham's town council agreed to allow use of a bridge over the Thames River. When the railway workers went ahead anyway, the Mayor, George W. Cowan, called in the fire department who used their hoses to chase the construction crew from the bridge. The company was allowed temporary use of the bridge, provided they remove the tracks after four months should no agreement be reached by then. Eventually the Chatham council approved of the route, and the tracks were laid.

In 1908 the route was extended to the lake at Erie Beach, and in 1909 a branch to Paincourt was added. While the beach line was mainly for the tourists and excursionists, the Paincourt branch was used to ship sugar beets from the farms in the area.

For most of its length, the route followed existing roads. From its station opposite the Wallaceburg town hall, the right of way paralleled the Pere Marquette line, then angled across country to follow the east shoulder of Baldoon Road. It entered Chatham on St Clair St and then followed Third, King and William Sts. through town. Its main power house, now demolished, stood at the northeast corner of King and Third. To leave Chatham the tracks then followed William to Queen which, upon leaving the city, becomes the Charing Cross Road.

At Charing Cross, an historic crossroads community, the railway had to literally tunnel under the tracks of the Michigan Central Railway, before continuing south to its destination, the park and pavilion at Erie Beach, a long sandy spit stretching into Lake Erie.

By the 1920s motor vehicles began puttering along the streets of Chatham putting pressure on the city council to pave the roads. When council began to pave over the CWLE's tracks, the company knew the end was near. While sugar beet shipments remained strong, passenger traffic dwindled, until, in 1930, the City of Chatham forced the CWLE to remove its poles and wires. The days of the CWLE were over.

 **All Aboard** _____

Because most of the route was along the shoulder of existing roads, vestiges are few. From Wallaceburg the route ran parallel to Wallace St and River Road before angling across the level fields to the Baldoon Road. The tracks followed the east shoulder of the dirt road coming to the hamlet of Electric and the intersection with CR 42. Electric was established by the CWLE as a shipping point for the railway and may be the only community in Ontario named after a radial railway line. While no buildings survive that tied directly to railway operations, the setback of the hall on the northeast corner reflects the right of way.

Three intersections south, the hamlet of Dover Centre contains one of the few direct vestiges of the railway, an elevator for the storage of the sugar beets which provided the CWLE with so much of its revenue. While fields have overtaken most of the roadbed, old stone abutments remain beside the drainage ditch on the southeast corner of Baldoon Road and Pioneer Road.

To reach Paincourt, follow Pioneer Road west to CR 43, the Bearline Rd, and take it north a short distance to Paincourt Line then west to Paincourt. Along the road, the CWLE roadbed is occasionally evident on the north shoulder. While the landmark elevator which stood in Paincourt by the track is long gone, the old hotel, beside which the trains once stopped, still stands.

Sadly, much of Chatham's history has been insensitively bulldozed. The few features which remain to see include the new museum, the black history museum, and the revitalized riverfront. Nothing, however, remains of the old electric railway which the councillors so despised.

From Chatham follow CR 10 to Erie Beach. While no evidence of the road bed survives by the roadside, the site of the tunnel beneath the MC at Charing Cross is marked by rubble on the west side of the road at the crossing. Also gone is the old store by which the trains once stopped.

The feed mill at Dover Centre is one of the few vestiges of the Chatham, Wallaceburg and Lake Erie Radial Railway.

Near Lake Erie, the community of Cedar Springs stretches along a prominent ridge, a feature which posed yet another impediment for the CWLE. Here the builders placed an embankment up to the ridge a short distant west of CR 10. From the embankment, which is still evident on the north side of today's CR 3, the right of way can be seen angling across the farm fields.

Finally, at Erie Beach, the tracks were located along today's main street. But here, too, all evidence of the area's railway heritage has been removed. The pavilion which stood into the 1980s in the former lakeside park, now a bible camp, has been removed. One structure which dates from train time, is the old stone hotel located at the western end of 4th Street.

The London and Lake Erie Railway: London to Port Stanley

Mention railways in Port Stanley, and nearly everyone knows of the Port Stanley Terminal Railway or as it was originally known, the London and Port Stanley. Today it operates as a busy tourist line. But mention that Port Stanley once had two railways, and all but the most knowledgeable locals will look puzzled.

However, there indeed was an interurban route between London

A radial streetcar from the London and Port Stanley Railway still operates on the grounds of the popular Electric Railway Museum near Rockwood.

and the lake and it was known as the Southwestern Traction Company (later as the London and Lake Erie Transportation Company.) Not only did it carry passengers, but it handled freight, and, in particular, fresh fish right off the boats in Port Stanley harbour. Its terminal was an indifferent cement block building on Main Street, just south of the main intersection. It was located behind the Clifton Hotel, where a short spur line led to the docks for passengers transferring to a steamer.

During the first world war, the LPS decided to electrify its line, as coal was in short supply. Because of its more direct route into London, the LPS could travel the route in 55 minutes, while the more circuitous LLE took an hour and three quarters. To further compound its problems, the LLE, being a provincially chartered electric line, was subject to the restrictive Lord's Day Act, and prohibited from operating on Sundays. The federally chartered LPS, on the other hand, was spared such a hindrance. By 1918, the LLE was broke and vanished from the landscape.

Its route took it along the now widened and much travelled Highway 4 the entire way into Port Stanley, before branching off onto Main Street. It is on Main Street, a short distance south of the intersection, that the little cement block station still stands. Although it

Erratum

On page 17, the final sentence is not complete. It should read:

"Although it bears little resemblance to a station, it remains the only evidence of this long lost and forgotten line"

2.

The Booze Line, Hiram Walker's Lake Erie and Detroit River Railway: St Thomas to Windsor

In 1856 American distiller Hiram Walker arrived on the Canadian side of the Detroit and began making booze, an operation which would ultimately become Canada's most prolific distillery. Around the distillery Walker laid out the planned community of Walkerville. By the 1880s the townsite had become one of Ontario's best planned communities with tree lined boulevards, attractive commercial buildings, such as the hotel and bank, and solid homes for the plant's workers. Walker's own company office has such appeal that it has been designated as a heritage structure.

And there was a railway station. In 1885 Walker brought into operation the Lake Erie and Detroit River Railway. Not only was it intended to bring the raw material from the farmlands south of Windsor to the distillery, but to export cattle and lumber north across the Detroit River to the American market. At first the line crossed only Essex County, reaching Leamington in 1889. But so great was the demand by the municipalities further east for a railway that by 1895 the route had been extended all the way to St Thomas. Here it met the Canada Southern Railway at a magnificent station built more than 20 years earlier.

From St Thomas, the LEDR had hoped to acquire the existing London and Port Stanley Railway, in order to have access to coal shipments arriving in Port Stanley from across Lake Erie. However, the City of London dithered so long over Walker's offer that the LEDR instead took over the operations of the Erie and Huron Railway with its Lake Erie port at Erieau. This also gave the LEDR connections through Chatham and north to Sarnia

At Erieau the LEDR built a large coaling facility and then entered the tourist business adding two excursion boats, the Shenango and Urania. These vessels operated between Conneaut Ohio and Erieau bringing tourists to stay at the popular Bungalow and Lakeview Hotels. With room for 200 guests, the Bungalow Hotel was the area's grandest hotel, but burned to the ground in 1912. It was never rebuilt. In 1972, the line to Erieau was the first portion of the LEDR to be abandoned.

Most of the stations along the line were constructed of wood, and displayed similar styles. Two, at Wheatley and Leamington, were given decorative octagonal towers above the bay, while the lakeside resort town of Kingsville was given the most attractive station on the line, a Richardsonian style stone station. The one in Walkerville was a large but boxy two-storey brick station.

Southwestern Ontario's main railway rivalries involved not Canadian but American interests. In 1904 to compete more aggressively against the American-owned Canada Southern, the Pere Marquette Railway took over the LEDR and operated it until 1951 when it became part of the Chesapeake and Ohio system, now the CSX.

For most of its route, the railway gained its business from the feed mills and grain elevators which loomed above the little station in nearly every town through which the line passed. Some fish were shipped from key fishing ports like Kingsville and Wheatley, while the major industry remained the distillery itself.

Gradually, international trucking interests won out over the railways, and the industries along the line switched to the more polluting and highway clogging form of transportation. Between 1992 and 1996 nearly the entire line between St Thomas and Walkerville was abandoned and the tracks lifted. The only track today is found in Windsor between the CN and CP lines, and in Blenheim where grain is moved northward along the former Erie and Huron track to Chatham.

 All Aboard --

St Thomas and Walkerville couldn't be more fitting termini for this route. With its railway heritage and landscape, St Thomas remains imbued in railway lore. Here sprawled the massive yards and railway shops of the Canada Southern Railway. The brick station, one of the

longest in Ontario, was built in 1873, and is destined for new use as a hotel and college residence.

Only a few rusting sidings now lie in the yards. Some of these, however, have become part of one of Ontario's most exciting railway museum, the Elgin County Railway Museum. Here, in the former engine house, a magnificent structure in its own right, is a display of historical railway rolling stock.

St Thomas is also now the northern terminus of the Port Stanley Terminal railway, a tourist train which operates from Port Stanley along the historic route of the London and Port Stanley Railway. For several years CN Rail, current owner of the CS, stubbornly and inexplicably refused the PST entry into St Thomas, and some negotiations are still ongoing over crossing rights.

At the west end of the town there stands another, albeit unusual, tribute to St Thomas' railway legacy, a life size statue of Jumbo. Said to

A postcard view shows the Canada Southern Station in St. Thomas, the eastern terminal of Hiram Walker's "Booze Line."

be the largest pachyderm ever in captivity, Jumbo was the highlight of PT Barnum's travelling circus. In 1885, following his nightly performance, Jumbo was being led along the track to his enclosure. The sudden approach of an unscheduled freight train panicked the beast who ran and stumbled, driving a tusk into his brain. Jumbo died soon after and was widely mourned. Following the accident, Barnum grotesquely displayed the hide for several years. Then in 1985, to commemorate the one hundredth anniversary of the event, the St Thomas Jumbo Foundation commissioned sculptor Winston Bronnum to create this life-size and life-like monument to what was probably the world's best loved elephant, and an integral part of Ontario's railway lore.

While visiting the Jumbo display, note the buildings in the vicinity. These represent St Thomas' original downtown area before the building of the CSR station to the east drew businesses in that direction.

To start this route follow Talbot St west from the Jumbo statue to Fingal Road, CR 16, and follow it west to the crossroads hamlet of Fingal. Turn north here following CR 20 north to Shedden. Here the two routes of the former railway rivals lie close together, the southerly of the two being the abandoned LEDR, the northerly being the Canada Southern. On the east side of the road, south of the former crossing, a small white farm house is the former Michigan Central station from the Canada Southern line.

Between Shedden and Highgate the two railway lines follow nearly adjacent rights of way.

From Shedden follow CR 3 for 6 ½ km west to Iona and there turn north onto CR 14 to Iona Station. A community which grew around the twin lines, Iona Station outgrew its parent hamlet and, despite the fact that trains no longer stop here, remains the larger of the two settlements. Another interesting feature in the area lies south of CR 3, a prehistoric fortification known as the Iona Earthworks. These aboriginal mounds lie along a path east of the road. While there is no admission fee, guides or facilities, on-site plaques explain the unusual feature.

From Iona Station drive north to CR 13 and west into Dutton. The presence of the two railways gave Dutton a prosperous main street, an appearance which it maintains to this day. The LEDR right of way has been grassed over, and the station and feed mill which still stood in the late 1980s are now both gone.

In Dutton drive to the north end of the village and follow CR 2 west to the next station stop, West Lorne.

West Lorne was another farm town that boomed when the railways, on adjacent rights of way, reached town. Again, however, all railway buildings have vanished, including the former station which, like that at Dutton, stood until the early 90s.

Continue west on CR 2 to Rodney and then north a short distance into the centre of town. Here a bit of the railway landscape has lingered. While the stations, once more, have been removed in recent years, an LEDR feed mill still towers over the vacant right of way, while an active feed mill still operates by the adjacent tracks of the Canada Southern. At the corner of Clarke St, north of the crossing, an attractive little railway hotel remains a community landmark.

The further west the route proceeds, the more prairie- like the landscape appears. The farmland becomes flatter, with fewer trees to mar the horizon. The wide main streets and the dominant feed mills give this region a decidedly western flavour. This is particularly so in Muirkirk, a small village, dusty and windblown, where feed mills dominate both railway routes. You can reach Muirkirk, 12 km west of Rodney, by following Elgin CR 104 and Kent CR 19. From Muirkirk a dirt road parallels the right of way, on the south side, and leads to the community of Highgate. Here, at the south end of the main street, loom the usual two feed mills, both operating. That by the LEDR now uses the right of way as a parking lot for the trucks that carry the feed.

West of Highgate, the two routes diverge, that of the CS entering Ridgetown about a half km north of the LEDR. To reach Ridgetown, drive north from the centre of Highgate back to CR 19 and follow it west for about 9 km to Erie St which leads south into Ridgetown crossing first the CSR. The right of way for the LEDR is closer to the centre of the village. Here finally stands a station. Although the line is abandoned, the building appears to still be a CSX communications facility.

Follow CR 19 west from Ridgetown for about 18 km to Blenheim.

By the time the LEDR and CSR reach Blenheim the two routes are more than five km apart. It comes as a surprise, after following an abandoned right of way this far, to see that trains still call at the row of massive feed mills beside the tracks in Blenheim. Pulled by small diesels, they are hauled northward along the former EH route to

Chatham. An attractive station with its decorative fretwork and hip gables, the Blenheim depot was demolished to provide more parking space for those trucks.

At the west end of Blenheim, CR 3 crosses the empty right of way of the LEDR's Erieau branch, although CR 12, a bit further west, is the most direct road route to the lake. Entering Erieau, the road splits on either side of a grassy boulevard which marks the former alignment of the rails into town. Now a busy resort and summer cottage community, Erieau offers no tribute to its railway roots. All evidence of the station and coal dock are gone, parks and a playground having taken their place.

From CR 12 follow CR 3 west for 18 km to CR 1 which leads north to Merlin. With its half ghosted main street, Merlin's more prosperous days vanished with the railway. The station stood here until the late 1980s when it disappeared, leaving the town, like so many others along this unfortunate railway line, without a fitting tribute to its own heritage. Such a dereliction is even more evident west of Merlin where farmers have ploughed the old right of way into oblivion.

The next station village, Glenwood, with a community hall and former store, is even closer to being a ghost town than is Merlin. To reach Glenwood, follow CR 8 northwesterly from Merlin for about 5 km to CR 14 which leads south to Glenwood.

Stevenson, a collection of homes and a church about a country intersection, retains no evidence of its railway days. To reach it, turn west at the intersection in Glenwood and drive to a T intersection. Turn right (keeping left at a fork in the road a short distance along) and travel the 2 km to CR 5 at Stevenson.

To reach Coatsworth, the next stop on the railway, follow CR 5 south to the 3rd Concession Line which is the second dirt road on the right, and follow for about 3 ½ km into Coatsworth. Here the land becomes increasingly prairie like as fields, flat and treeless stretch to the horizon. At Coatsworth, a feed mill guards the empty right of way, while a prairie-style false-fronted general store stands nearby. With its cracked sidewalks, the village's railway prosperity is now behind it.

The ghosts of the rail age are even fainter at Renwick where the feed mill and station are long gone, and only a pair of houses are left to indicate that any sort of community existed here at all. To reach the

The gaunt remains of a grain silo stand beside the Chrysler Canada Greenway at Oldcastle, one of the few remains of the trail's railway roots.

location, drive a short distance north from Coatsworth to the 3rd Concession, the first road on the left. Follow it west to CR 3 and Renwick which lies a short distance south. In both Coatsworth and Renwick, the right of way remains in an abandoned state, and has not been put to any alternate use at this writing.

From Renwick drive south to the 2nd Concession and follow it west until you reach CR 3, the Talbot Road. Wheatley lies about 6 km west.

Wheatley remains one of Lake Erie's premier fishing ports, and the station which was built here reflected that importance. Identical to that in Leamington, it was an attractive grey wooden building with an octagonal tower above the bay. However, it was demolished in the 1960s. The right of way now serves as a private lane and parking lot for the ever present feed mill. The only evidence that trains ever ran here is the former railway hotel on the west side of the road.

Although it is a bustling and attractive lakeside town, with access to Point Pelee National Park, and the last of the Lake Erie ferries, if you're looking for railway history, you won't find it in Leamington. Despite some concerted but fruitless efforts to save it, the Leamington station burned in 1998. "We expected it," sneered one local resident. Neither is the right of way evident. The only legacy of the railway is in

Despite local efforts to save it, the Leamington station burned down in 1998, another victim of heritage neglect.

the name of a nearby restaurant, the Sherman Station Restaurant.

Happily, the LEDR's heritage is more visible west of Leamington. While nothing remains near the former station grounds at Ruthven, the right of way becomes part of the Chrysler Canada Greenway near the popular Colasanti's Tropical Gardens. This hiking trail, completed in 1999, follows the LEDR route right across the warm lush farmlands of Essex County to the hamlet of Oldcastle on the fringe of Windsor. The trail is a lasting legacy to one its strongest proponents, former Chrysler Canada chairman G.Y. Landry, who died in 1998. Fittingly, the trail forms part of the 17,000 km (10,500 mile) Trans Canada Trail.

Despite this effort, the only surviving station along the trail is that at Kingsville. The grandest on the line, it was constructed of large field stones, with arched doorways, windows and porch. Built in 1889, it was designed by Detroit architects Mason and Rice, following a style then being made popular in the eastern U.S. by architect H.H. Richardson. Until a few years ago it retained its red tile roof, however, these were

removed in a failed private preservation effort. Today a job creation partnership involving the Town of Kingsville, the Essex Region Conservation Authority and Human Resources Canada is providing funds to restore the wonderful piece of railway history. (Conspicuous by its absence from this partnership is the provincial government.) The station is located on Lansdowne Ave south of Main Street.

The Kingsville station, LEDR's finest, will be restored as part of the Chrysler Canada Greenway.

From Kingsville, you can follow either the highway or the trail west for 16 km to the community of Harrow. Here on the former station grounds a "community entrance" provides access to the trail, with a parking lot. On a plaque describing the trail's ecology and railway history, you can read of the diverse landscapes along the route as it passes through farmlands, vineyards, wetlands and some of Ontario's few surviving Carolinian forests (some of which are, incredibly, being cleared for golf courses).

North and west of Harrow the trail crosses Cedar Creek and the Canard River valley. Here, you will see Carolinian landscapes and

The offices of the Hiram Walker distillery have been designated as an historic structure, and demonstrate Walker's aesthetic commitment to his adopted community.

southern plant and animal species, such as Kentucky coffee trees, found nowhere else in Canada. In fact, the trail links 25 separate natural areas, crossing six watersheds as it does so.

Sadly, the only thing missing, aside from the Kingsville station, is the legacy of the railway itself. Although a vacant feed mill still stands at Harrow, nothing whatever remains at either New Canaan or Paquette's Corners. On the south side of the highway at Oldcastle there still stands the gaunt remains of a feed mill, reflecting the vanishing farmlands of the rural areas around Windsor.

Oldcastle is the western terminus of the trail, with picnic grounds, a parking lot and information kiosk. CR 11 winds its way across the vanishing Essex County countryside to Oldcastle where the entrance to the trail is on the north side of Highway 3, just east of CR 11.

North of Oldcastle, CR 11 becomes Walker Road and parallels the LEDR through Windsor's unsightly sprawl right to the site of Walkerville and the distillery which brought about the railway in the first place. A short section of track remains in place between the CPR line, and the Conrail line, but becomes abandoned again closer to Walkerville itself where a now trackless bridge crosses Wyandott Rd.

Be warned, Walker Rd is not an attractive stretch of road, with strip development, sprawl and factories dominating. But that all changes when you reach Walkerville itself. From Walker Road, follow Richmond St west to Willistead Park where the Walker Family mansion has been preserved. Between the mansion and the river, the handsome homes of the company town dominate the streets, with the hotel, and bank building both attractive brick structures, lying close to the historic Walker company offices. Ironically, the C and O station burned in the early 90s, removing the last legacy of Walkerville's railway history.

3.

On To Kincardine, The Kincardine Branch of the Wellington Grey and Bruce: Listowel to Kincardine

The first concerted effort to link Toronto with Lake Huron by rail was made by the Wellington Grey and Bruce Railway, completed between Guelph and Southampton in December of 1872 (please refer to *Ghost Railways of Ontario: Volume One*). Almost immediately work began on another branch. Despite being close to Southampton on the Lake Huron shore, Kincardine was to become a second lakeside terminus for the WGB. From the WGB hub at Palmerston, construction snaked across country in 1873, twisting and winding to ensure that all subscriber communities had a station.

Talk of extending the line to Owen Sound was soon dismissed. However, in 1876, the London Huron and Bruce was completed from London to meet the WGB at Wingham Junction.

Most of the products shipped along the line were, as would be expected, agricultural, with salt being mined and shipped from Kincardine. Passenger service continued on the line until 1970. Then, in 1983, the line was cut back from Kincardine to Wingham and in 1993 from Wingham to Palmerston itself. The rail era in the Grey-Bruce region of Ontario was over.

 **All Aboard** ------------------------------------

While few railway buildings remain on the route, this trip passes through some of Ontario's more purely rural communities. Most trace their boom period to the arrival of the WGB, and in some cases have changed little since. No Wal Marts or big box stores here. Following this line is a true country drive, ending at the blue waters of Lake Huron.

One of the two stations still in place on this route is that at Listowel. Now known as the Kinsman Station, it is located at the corner of Victoria St and Binning three blocks north of the main street. The original main line of the Stratford and Huron Railway(see Chapter 4) met the Kincardine branch where the right of way currently crosses Main Street, and then passed a few metres west of the later track. The former CPR station, a handsome brick building, stood on Wallace Street south of Main Street. Although it had found a new use as a Hydro office, it was nonetheless demolished in the late 1980s.

For a time, the GT planned to replace its wooden station with a more elaborate brick building, similar in design to that still standing in Southampton. However, those plans were not followed through, and the station which you see here is still the old wooden one. Although it has been little altered on the outside, the interior has been changed to accommodate its new role.

From Listowel, the WGB parallels Highway 23, on the east side, south to Atwood. Here, near the south end of town, the wide right of way bends west to cross the road. However, except for a former loading dock, no evidence of the railway's heritage has survived here.

From Atwood, drive south to CR 72, Newry Road, and drive west. The WGB parallels this road about 1 km to the north. Now a ghost town, Henfryn, a short distance north of Newry Road on Henfryn Line, was a busy shipping point for farm products, and bricks manufactured in a nearby brickyard. Although small, the station contained a waiting room and an apartment for the agent. Following its closure in the 1960s, it was moved to a nearby farm. Now, only foundations and a couple of early homes mark the site of this nearly vanished railway hamlet.

At this point the road crosses from Perth County into Huron County and becomes CR 16. From Henfryn, continue west on CR 16 to Ethel Line. Here the WGB passed south of the village of Ethel, where a small station and siding were placed. Although all evidence of the siding and station have long vanished, Ethel remains a busy rural settlement. The site of the siding lies a few meters north of CR 16.

Continue west along CR 16 into the community of Brussels. Here still stands a number of solid brick main street stores, a small mill, and the station. The right of way crosses CR 12 a short distance north of

the downtown area where, beside the fair grounds and the lawn bowling club, now rests the simple but elegant CN style station. It replaced a much larger GT station which had been built in 1899.

To reach Bluevale, the WGB's next station stop, continue north on CR 12 to CR 86 and drive west. Bluevale lies south of the highway just past the intersection with CR 87. Here a number of older rural buildings still stand, among them the old grist mill. The right of way crosses the road about a kilometre south of the mill, but most evidence of the route here has vanished. Despite the small size of the community, the GT replaced the original WGB station with a full sized station of its own.

Now lost in the rural sprawl which emanates from Wingham lies Wingham Junction where the tracks of the London Huron and Bruce met those of the WGB. Here, around the little station, the wye and the sidings, a small community developed. After 1941, following the abandonment of the LHB from Wingham Junction to Clinton, most evidence of this historic link vanished. Only a few older homes on the

The first station built in Brussels was eventually replaced. The new one has been relocated to the local lawn bowling club.

The Wingham station, shown here before the tracks were lifted, has now been restored for community use.

north side of the highway indicate that here there once stood something more than today's rural sprawl.

Wingham today is a bustling rural centre with new businesses expanding along CR 86. Downtown Wingham, with several blocks of historic businesses, lies north of 86 along CR 4, the London Road. A few blocks beyond the northern limit of downtown, sits one of the most unusual of Ontario's small town stations. Built by the GT in 1906, two gangly towers stood on each side of the station entrance which faced the street, while tracks lay on both sides of the building. Close by were the typical terminal facilities of the engine house, coaling facilities and crew bunkhouse.

After CN cut the line back from Kincardine, Wingham remained for several years the end of the line. During this time, the towers were reduced in height and then the station sat empty and deteriorating. Today it has been carefully restored and is used as a community building. However, all other evidence of the railway has gone.

From Wingham the WGB continued west, the right of way paralleling CR 86 a short distance north. The station area at Whitechurch, about 8 km west of Wingham, consisted of a grain elevator, cattle sheds and a combination station. The right of way, about a kilometre north

In Lucknow, only a grain elevator survives from the days of rail. In the foreground the station grounds are vacant.

of the main intersection in town, now contains no evidence of these structures.

The next stop, Lucknow, lies nine km west of Whitechurch and had one of the larger stations on the route. Here, after leaving Whitechurch, the route bent towards the north west and crossed CR 1 about a km north of CR 86. A couple of blocks east of CR 1 stood the station, cattle yards, and a large grain elevator. Today the station grounds are vacant and overgrown, with no trace of even the platform. Immediately to the south, however, the grain elevator still looms above the weeds, and continues to be both a landmark and a legacy to a forgotten railway heritage. Its fate, however, remains uncertain.

From Lucknow continue north on CR 1 to CR 6 and follow it west to Ripley. While several old commercial buildings still stand in Ripley's downtown, the old board and batten station is not among them. A busy feed mill still reflects the community's historic ties to its farming roots.

The terminus of the Kincardine branch lies in the shifting sands of a Lake Huron beach. Here stood an engine house, cattle yards, coal yards and an attractive yellow brick station. Beside the harbour a small

The Ripley station reflects the style employed at most local stations on the Kincardine Branch.

wooden lighthouse guided fishing boats and schooners from Huron's open waters into the shelter of the port. The arrival of the rails brought with it such industries as the Malcolm Furniture company, the Circle Bar Knitting Company and a wicker factory. For a few years, a salt mine operated near the beach.

Following the closing of the line the terminal facilities were removed and the station burned. Today the site has been rejuvenated as an attractive park. Parking, picnicking and bathing have replaced the hissing and puffing of railway days. A boardwalk parallels the right of way along the beach, where informational plaques outline the ecology of the small dunes. A short distance south of the parking lot, the right of way itself remains clearly visible. Closer to the marina, a small facility has been built to vaguely resemble the old station house. But the only truly historic structure to survive by the port is the picturesque wooden lighthouse, which is now a museum. If you're passing this way in the summer, leave enough time to enjoy the Bluewater Summer Festival Theatre.

While there are many opportunities to enjoy summer on the entire coastline of Lake Huron, very little of the lakeshore is open to the public, or even visible from the road. One of the more photogenic historic

landmarks is the Point Clark lighthouse. Now a national historic site, this elegant stone tower was built in the Imperial Style, one of six built on Lake Huron and Georgian Bay between 1855 and 1859. It is located west of Highway 21 about 17 km south of Kincardine.

The pretty little brick station in Kincardine, shown here after the tracks were removed, was also slated for re-use before it was destroyed by fire.

4.

From William Shakespeare to Wiarton Willie, The Stratford and Huron Railway: Stratford to Wiarton

During the heady railway boom years of the 1870s, communities all across Ontario dreamed of becoming major railway towns. Stratford, far from any port, was no exception. As early as the 1850s, the Stratford business community began to lobby for a rail link from their fledgling town to Southampton on Lake Huron. This, along with proposals for the Port Dover and Lake Huron Railway, which would connect with Lake Erie, could put Stratford on a busy portage railway.

However, optimism gave way to reality. Funds could not be found, and the project was delayed. Finally, in 1877, construction on the SHR began between Stratford and Listowel, a mill town on the Maitland River a few miles north. By this time, Southampton had fallen firmly within the grip of the rival Wellington Grey and Bruce Railway, operated by the Great Western, and the SHR terminus was changed to the more northerly Wiarton.

There was even talk of continuing the line beyond that, and right up the barren Bruce Peninsula to Tobermory, with a link to Manitoulin Island. But that, too, fell by the wayside.

Finances continued to plague the SHR. In 1880 the promoters were forced to go, cap in hand, to the Grand Trunk, the Great Western's main rival, to ask for help. In taking over the railway, the GT forced the SHR to build a branch into Palmerston, then a budding railway junction. At the same time the name was changed to the Grand Trunk Georgian Bay and Lake Erie Railway, to reflect the other lines the GT had assumed as well. Under the new name, track laying continued to Wiarton, and in July 1882, the new line was open.

In 1882 the Great Western and the Grand Trunk amalgamated, and

The beautiful "witch's hat" station at Chesley was demolished when the CN no longer needed it.

the network of lines emanating spoke-like from Palmerston suddenly came under the same ownership. Almost immediately, a new, more direct link was built from Palmerston to Listowel, and this short section of the original main line was abandoned. Then, in 1891, a branch line was built from Park Head into Owen Sound to a terminus immediately opposite that occupied by the rival Toronto Grey and Bruce, CP's link to Georgian Bay. As the SHR already had a terminus on Georgian Bay, this new branch was built to serve the Shallow Lake Cement Plant founded by R.J. Doyle. Here, the chalky deposits on the floor of the shallow lake proved ideal for the manufacture of cement.

As with most early railways, the first stations were tediously simple designs. Typical of the structures along the SHR, stations were squat wide buildings, with a bay window, if there was one at all, at the corner. Around the turn of the century, the GT upgraded many of its lines, and replaced its earlier depots with far more imposing structures. The new stations along the old SHR shared common characteristics. These included towers, a high Dutch gable above the bay window and steeply-pitched hip gable roofs. Two examples of this style were found at Harriston and Hanover.

Chesley was given special treatment with not only a small tower above the entrance, but with a "witch's hat," a soaring conical roof above the waiting room. While the station at Wiarton was enhanced by a tower and a rounded waiting room, it was not given a conical roof.

With the advent of the auto age, service was gradually cut back. In 1957 mail was no longer carried and in 1958 the line to Wiarton was abandoned. Then, in 1970, passenger service to Owen Sound ceased and finally, in 1995 the line was abandoned, and the rails subsequently lifted.

 All Aboard --

The route starts in Stratford, and winds north through Milverton and Listowel, and then into the one time rail hub of Palmerston. It then heads north through some of Ontario's best farmland into Hanover and onward to Chesley, Wiarton and Owen Sound. Here are communities that cling tenaciously to their rural roots, small towns with solid bustling main streets, and historical structures which link to the past. Sadly, most of the best railway stations have been removed, notably those at Hanover (to make way for a parking lot) and at Chesley. Those at Milverton, Listowel, Palmerston, Elmwood, Wiarton and Owen Sound, however, have all been saved, although three were relocated to new sites.

While much of Stratford's railway legacy has gone, the station still survives and, indeed, still sees four passenger trains a day on the Toronto to Sarnia and Toronto to Chicago runs. The once extensive yards still sprawl before the stone station, but now they hold only the engines of RailTex's Goderich short line. Gone too are the engine shops, the greenhouses and the once familiar railway YMCA.

The station is located on (what else?) Shakespeare Street just south of the attractively preserved downtown core. Stratford has much to offer besides its railway history. The annual Shakespearean Festival brings in plays and many visitors and the landscaped parks are a stroller's paradise.

To leave town along the route of the SHR, follow Romeo Street north. At the Stratford Festival theatre, look for the still surviving trestle across the Avon River. At Vivian Street turn left to CR 119 and fol-

The former station hotel, and the feed mill recall the lost railway days in Brunner.

low it north. Gad's Hill Siding, a short distance west of CR 119 immediately north of the highway village of Gad's Hill, consisted of only a small shelter where cans of milk were occasionally left for the train crew to pick up.

CR 119 continues north and then bends west, passing through the hamlet of Brunner. Although small, the community contained stockyards, lumber and coal yards, a creamery, cheese factory and grain elevator. While the station and most of the trackside industries are gone, the elevator and the station hotel, still named as such, provide a link with Brunner's railway legacy.

From Brunner, CR 119 becomes CR 131 and continues on into the solidly rural town of Milverton, a community where the horses and buggies of the area's Mennonite farmers clop along the streets. Milverton once enjoyed two railway lines; now it has none. The route of the Guelph and Goderich, a CP line, crossed the main street a short distance north of the main intersection, while that of the SHR passed well to the east of the main street.

Turn east onto Mill St. at the main intersection and drive for more than a kilometer. Just as the residences on the street seem to be petering out, a few older ones appear to mark the site of the former crossing. The station, a replacement built by CN in 1937, was moved to a nearby Mennonite farm, where it remains in good condition, and is used for storage.

A short distance beyond the crossing, turn left onto Road 129 and continue to Perth Line 72 and the village of Newton. Halfway between Milverton and Newton, a short distance west along Perth Line 67, the bridge abutments which carried the G and G over the SHR, still stand. In Newton, the crossing was located at the west end of the village, where a large feed mill and a few commercial buildings, including a one-time hotel, still recall the days of rail.

Continue west on Perth Line 72 to rejoin CR 131. Follow it north to the next crossroads, Line 75, and turn left again to the first crossroads and the little hamlet of Peffers. Here stood a small flag station along with coal and cattle yards. The road through Peffers continues west to Road 147 which leads north to the next little station, Britton. But here, again, no evidence remains of the community's railway days.

Listowel, however, is a different story. The massive wooden station, built in 1873, has been preserved and now serves various Kinsmen functions. It lies west of Barber St and north of CR 86. Prior to the 1882 merger of the GT and GW, the station stood further south, at the site of the junction itself, along with a turntable and two stall round-house. Like many of the area's towns, Listowel is a bustling place, with solid rural roots.

From Listowel, Highway 23 leads north through Gowanston, which once had an early station, to the remarkable former railway hub of Palmerston. Although its days of rail are long gone, Palmerston has clung to its railway heritage. The two-storey wooden station, with its truncated tower, has been restored and the historic footbridge crosses the yards to where a steam engine is on display. In the silent yards, some rail remains in place where it is hoped Palmerston's popular annual hand car races can continue to occur.

In Palmerston drive to the east end of the village and follow CR 5 north to CR 109 and then west into Harriston. This represents the Southampton Branch of the WGB as well as the Wiarton main line of the SHR, and is discussed in *Ghost Railways of Ontario Volume One*. Here, the Harriston station, minus tracks and now a seniors drop-in centre, still stands, and is situated on Highway 89 a little west of Highway 9.

The station in Palmerston was the centre of a busy divisional yard. While the trains no longer call, the station has been restored.

From Harriston, drive west for about 4 km on Highway 9 and turn north onto Ayton Rd which becomes CR 3. At CR 2, drive west a short distance into the hamlet of Drew where the old general store still operates beside the abandoned right of way.

Return to CR 3 and continue north. A short distance west of the intersection of CR 3 and Concession 6, the whistle stop of Alsfeldt once contained a blacksmith, carriage shop, cheese factory, store and hotel.

CR 3 continues on north to the interesting little farm town of Ayton. The right of way crosses the road on an angle two km west of the village, where the station stood at the end of a dirt track named Station Road. The village itself is an historic treasure trove, with old stores, hotels, and even blacksmith shops (no longer used as such) that reflect its rural heritage. Unfortunately, the old station did not share that good fortune.

From Ayton, follow CR 9 west to Sideroad 5, the first crossroads. Then turn right and drive 4 km into Neustadt. Another bonanza of historic structures, the village contains the historic Commercial Hotel, its landmark stone brewery, and the birthplace of former prime minister John Diefenbaker. Sadly, the railway heritage has been lost, the station having been relocated only to burn down. At the former crossing only the railway hotel, at this writing a closed-up restaurant, marks the spot. In its heyday, Neustadt was a major rail shipper sending out lumber, furniture, farm products, and, of course, beer.

Once a busy furniture town, Hanover, the next station stop, has become the commercial hub of the county. New malls, a growing main street, and new industries give the place an aura of expansion. But prosperity has come with a price. In order to expand the parking area for the New Life Mills, the classic and historic Grand Trunk station was demolished. Even the original SHR station, a small board and batten building, stood on a lot north of the tracks until it disappeared in the late '80s. It was the last of the original SHR stations.

A small section of the right of way has become a community trail commencing on the west side of Bruce Road and extending south to Concession 2, SDR. But this is only a small concession to a railway heritage that in Hanover has been ignored and, now, lost.

Perhaps Elmwood, about 10 km north of Hanover on CR 10, has missed out on the growth enjoyed by its southerly neighbour to remain a functional yet featureless farm village. Its station, however, unlike that at Hanover, has survived. It was relocated to Concession 12, a short distance to the north and has been converted to a dwelling, retaining many of its exterior features.

Chesley, once a thriving industrial town, with mills and furniture factories, like the Heirloom Factory, is losing its economic base. It does, however, retain much of this heritage, with mills still standing, and functioning on water power. Seventh Street leads west from CR 10 to the site of the station, a witch's hat building now sadly gone. A freight shed, however still stands nearby. Second Street leads west to the large iron bridge which carried the trains high above the North Saugeen River. A short distance further along sits one of those hidden heritage treasures, a board and batten grist mill which still grinds grain using the water power of the river.

A further 12 km north along CR 10 leads to Dobbinton, the SHR's next station stop. A small rural hamlet, Dobbinton's main export was cattle. The right of way is blocked off, while all other evidence of the community's railway heritage has vanished.

At Tara, the right of way crosses CR 10 near the south end of town.

The old board and batten station at Neustadt, now gone, was typical of many along the SHR.

Prior to the arrival of the railway, Tara was in fact two former stage coach villages: Tara, situated north of the Sauble River, and Invermay on the south. However, the SHR located south of the river, and adopted the name Tara. Here, where the 1901 Grand Trunk stood, along with a milk processing plant, industry now occupies the site.

CR 10 comes to a T intersection at Highway 21 about 6 km north of Tara and a short distance east of where the Allenford station stood. The village of Allenford itself is about 2 km further west. Follow Highway 21 east to the continuation of CR 10, then north to Park Head. The right of way, now a snowmobile trail, is marked by a couple of early commercial buildings, and a few railway-era houses. This was the point from which the branch line into Owen Sound was built from the Wiarton main line.

From Park Head north to Wiarton the old right of way has been abandoned for more than 40 years. At Hepworth, the next stop on the former main line, the Grand Trunk replaced the original SHR station with one of its standard plans for the area, one which displayed an octagonal gable above a similarly designed bay window. The relocated Cargill station, on the Southampton branch, and about 15 km northwest of Walkerton, is the only surviving example of this plan. Products shipped from this point included lumber and cement.

From Hepworth north to Clavering, the right of way is visible on the east side of the highway, passing behind the historic landmark general store in the hamlet of Clavering.

Wiarton, the original terminus of the SHR, is now a busy tourist town, gateway to the Bruce Peninsula, and birthplace of the late (and lamented) Wiarton Willie, and his successor, Wee Wiarton Willie, Ontario's harbinger of spring. The main railway exports here were cement, lumber, sugar beets and, later, fish. After the last train rolled out in 1958, the station was moved from its original location at George and Claude Sts to Bluewater Park where it has been restored and now serves as a park office. All other evidence that Wiarton was ever a key railway town has vanished.

With the closing of the Wiarton branch, Owen Sound took over as the terminus, although it had been gaining in importance even before that. At Shallow Lake, the site of cement export, the station site lies just west of Highway 6.

From there to Owen Sound, the line passed by a pair of flag stops named Murphys and Benallen, before winding down the Niagara Escarpment and into Owen Sound. The first station in Owen Sound was a simple low-roofed structure located on the west side of the harbour on First Avenue. It was replaced in 1932 with a CN plan station that included a gable above the bay.

Beside the docks the railway connected with ships carrying cattle and grain, while local industries served by the railway included Kennedy and Sons Foundry, Northern Paint and Varnish, Harrisons Lumber Mill and RCA Victor. The CN linked with the CP line on the south side of 10th Street. Happily, Owen Sound's railway days have not entirely died as the station survives now as a marine museum. Unfortunately, the sound of the train whistle is no longer heard anywhere along the route of the SHR.

Owen Sound, despite its urban sprawl, is attractively situated on the fjord-like bay. The Bruce Trail passes through the western and southern sections of town, leading hikers along craggy clifftops to the plunging waters of Inglis Falls. Despite the loss of both railways, the port of Owen Sound still sees the looming lake freighters glide beneath the cliffs of the Niagara Escarpment and rumble to a halt at one of the docks. Several motels and restaurants offer the traveller ample opportunity to rest after a long day on the old SHR.

5.

The St Mary's and Western: Ingersoll to St Mary's

Like so many other grandly named railways in Ontario's early years, the St. Mary's and Western lived up to only part of its name. Its charter, granted in 1905, called for it to build from a point on the CP line between Woodstock and London, to the St Clair River between Grand Bend and Sarnia. What it would do after that seemed to be anybody's guess, although several lines on the Michigan side did reach the St Clair at various places.

Instead, the line ended up at St Mary's, living out its life as a branch to the burgeoning CPR network. Although short, the route passes through some of southern Ontario's most attractive farm country and rural villages before terminating at St. Mary's, one of the province's most stunning stone cities. Abandoned in 1995, little has been preserved along this route and it is yet another depressing example of local communities ignoring their railway heritage.

 All Aboard ---

The route begins in Ingersoll beside a one-time railside factory, now a recycling depot, on the east end of town. (Before starting, visit the town's original Great Western station beside the VIA shelter at the CN crossing a short distance west of Oxford County Road 119.)

From the factory take Zorra 33rd Line north to CR 2. Lined for a part of its route with hydro poles, the right of way sits disused. Turn right to drive to Zorra and turn left onto the 35th Line where the extensive Lefarge extraction operation dominates the landscape, and has covered over the SMW right of way. After less than ½ km you come to a still active CPR line. Although freight trains still rumble through

Near Embro, this small bridge once carried the tracks of the SMW.

on the CP's main line, the old wooden Zorra station has long been gone, its grounds now the site of a communications tower.

North of Zorra, the right of way parallels the road to the west, scarcely visible in a corn field. It crosses to the east side just beyond Road 74, where it is a farm lane. Turn right here and travel to CR 6 where you turn left. The right of way crosses CR 6 a little more than a km along. Then, at the next crossroads, CR 33, turn right to the railway roadbed, and look for an old bridge on the south side of the road. Then, return back to the intersection which is the south end of the village of Embro

Embro, which is an ancient pronunciation of the name Edinborough, offers a wider than usual main street which leads to the right of way, here a laneway by the north branch of the Thames River. The station grounds were not here, but rather at the north end of the village on the east side of CR 6, where they are now largely obliterated by a small housing development.

Portions of the right of way north west of Embro remain visible, while others have been sold to adjacent farms and ploughed from history. Turn west from CR 6 just north of Embro and onto CR 16. Drive about 7 km, to the 6th crossroad, which is the 26th Line, and turn

The station at Lakeside now sits in a local church yard.

right to drive to Lakeside, the site of the SMW's only surviving station.

After five km the road bends around the little lake, where a few summer homes have been built, and enters the centre of the old hamlet. In the yard beside Christ Anglican Church sits the small white frame building that is the former station. Little altered on the outside, it was one of those almost ubiquitous "Swiss Cottage" styles that the CPR placed in many communities during the 1930s.

Turn left at the main intersection in Lakeside onto CR 25, where an old general store still stands, and a few meters further along the right of way itself crosses, visible on the south side, but ploughed under on the north.

Follow CR 25 west to CR 119, which in turn leads north to St Marys.

At one point in its history, St Marys enjoyed the use of three railway stations: that in the centre of town on the Grand Trunk's main line, that at St Mary's Junction a short distance north of town marking the historic route of the Grand Trunk west to Sarnia, and that of the SMW, a small wooden building located just south of St Mary's historic stone bridge.

Of the three, only that of the SMW has been demolished, typically, by the CPR. The junction station, an ancient original GT stone station

St Mary's attractive little SMW station was removed to make way for a parking lot.

built in 1858, sits plaqued as a national historic site, and is protected by a chain link fence, but is otherwise appallingly neglected, a disgrace to its stewards. The SMW station, which stood until the early 1990s, was removed to make room for a potholed parking lot, while the right of way has, more constructively, been asphalted to become a walkway along the river. The GT's pretty downtown station, built of yellow brick, still enjoys VIA Rail service.

They don't call St Mary's the stone city for nothing. Many of its main street buildings, the most magnificent of which is the post office, are constructed of beautiful white stone.

To reach St Marys follow CR 119 to Highway 7 where you cross the through the intersection and continue to a T intersection with CR 9 which leads west into town, becoming Queen St.

As you cross over the tracks on a bridge, you can see the current station below you to the right. To reach the historic junction station follow Wellington north from Queen St to Station St. Then, watch for Glass St and turn right. The station is only a short distance along.

Queen and Water Sts represent the main intersection in town, where many of the town's finest structures are located. You can find the site of the SMW station and the walkway along the river by turning south onto Water St and entering the parking lot beside the river opposite Elgin St.

St Mary's is a pretty and strollable little town. Several historic structures line its busy streets, among them ancient stone stores and the landmark opera house. Beneath the photogenic stone arch bridge, recently reconstructed to handle more traffic, the river rushes over layers of limestone. Perhaps after enjoying some non-railway heritage, you might catch a real train home.

6.

Across the Roof of Ontario, the Toronto Grey and Bruce: Orangeville to Owen Sound

Clouds scudded low over the flat pasture lands. The winds blew strong and cold from the north west and the snow began to fall. The howling gale blew the sheets of snow sideways so that one farm could not be seen from the next. The blizzard blew for days on end, long grey days which stretched into weeks. By the time the snow drifts had reached the tops of the telegraph poles, it had snowed for 70 days without a break. It was the winter of 1875, the one which trapped a train for six weeks in an immense snow drift. It was the first such delay due to weather, but it would not be the last. Many present and former residents recall the winter of 1947 when drifts again buried trains, and kept children from travelling to school for up to two weeks.

Such was the land which the Toronto Grey and Bruce had to endure.

Interest in a railway to Owen Sound had surfaced as early as 1850 when the Toronto and Sydenham Railway, and the Northern Railway both approached the town for help in financing a line. Such a route would, they surmised, tap into the lush forests and fledgling farms as well as divert Great Lakes shipping through new rail heads on Lake Huron and Georgian Bay. But the community refused, confident that the railway would eventually be forced to build there anyway. What they hadn't counted on was that the rival Simcoe County was prepared to ante up the money. As a result, the Northern Railway snubbed Owen Sound, and built their line instead to Collingwood. The town would wait another two decades before they heard their first train whistle.

The 1868 charter for a railway, known as the Toronto Grey and Bruce, allowed for a line from Toronto to Mount Forest and Durham via Orangeville. From Mount Forest branches would extend north to

Owen Sound and west to Southampton. Although the route reached Mount Forest in 1871, neither of the branches materialized as envisioned. In 1873 the County of Grey again backed out of its funding commitments, and the branch from Mount Forest to Owen Sound was scrapped. Meanwhile, the proposed main line stalled at Teeswater, well short of the waters of Lake Huron.

But the promoters were adamant to have a lake terminal. As a result they relocated their junction to Orangeville and built their Owen Sound branch northwesterly from that point. The land over which they laid their rails was flat, with few obstacles, and the first train puffed into the bay side station in 1873.

Most of the first stations on the route were single-storey board and batten buildings, those needing agents' quarters were two storeys. Most were replaced following the turn of the century with single storey buildings, larger, and better built, with more attractive architecture detailing.

The route proved to be prosperous. Grain was trans-shipped at the busy port, while cattle clomped into the cattle cars from many of the communities through which the line passed, and those which the line created. Passenger service lasted nearly a century, ending only in 1970 (although many today wish it were still in place). Then, in 1995, following failed attempts to sell to a short line owner, the legendary line was abandoned and three years later the rails lifted. As of this writing, the right of way remains abandoned, its disposal undecided. In keeping with CPR policy, no station, except that at Owen Sound remains on site. Only three, Shelburne, Crombies, and Markdale were moved, the latter now collapsed through lack of care.

While freights occasionally still travel as far as Orangeville, north of that the line is gone. (The "main line" or the Teeswater Branch was featured in *Ghost Railways of Ontario: Volume One*.)

 **All Aboard** --

This route starts in Orangeville, either at the station- restaurant, or at the restaurant-station. Because of its location, Orangeville was chosen as a divisional point. Here sorting yards were laid out, an engine

This bridge still stands on the TGB right of way north of Shelburne.

house, coal dock and water tank were added, and a restaurant was built. Most divisional points had an eatery, for while the trains underwent their mandatory servicing, and the crew changed shifts, the passengers could crowd into the little café for a quick meal. In Orangeville, the one-time divisional restaurant is the only building left in the divisional yards, and today serves as a station of sorts for the few crew still employed here. Hence it can be called a restaurant-station. The station itself, meanwhile, was moved to Mill Street to become—a restaurant. Built in 1906, it was, with its conical roof above the waiting room (a style nick-named the "witch's hat") and its wood shingle siding, the handsomest station on the line.

Today the track extends only a short distance beyond the former station grounds. At the site of Fraxa Junction, located on the Third Line a short distance north of Grey Road 109, only the gravel right of way remains to mark the route.

Between Fraxa and Shelburne, the right of way parallels the Third Line which extends from County Road 109 to Crombies, where the Third Line becomes Dufferin Road 12. Three little flag stops stood along the way, at Framingham, Laurel and Crombies. At the latter station, the architects embellished the tiny shed with an attractive overall

Above: Train time is depicted on a mural painted on the side of a store in downtown Dundalk.

Left: A pair of feed mills still straddle the abandoned right of way in Dundalk.

appearance, and fluting in the board and batten roof. The building survives today in the Dufferin County Museum at Airport Road and Highway 89.

A practical looking farm town, and home of one of North America's paramount fiddling contests, Shelburne looks much as it did during rail days. A mural on a downtown building depicts train time at the station, while a feed mill still stands on the silent right of way. The station itself was built in 1914 as part of an overall station replacement program along the line, replacing a simpler two-storey wooden structure. A single storey wooden structure patterned after most of the others, it was moved away to become a private home where its owners have taken care to preserve the station's exterior appearance. It is located about 10 km southeast of Shelburne.

Highway 10 parallels the right of way north of Shelburne where the next station, Melancthon, is now a ghost town with only a general store to mark the site. The right of way and site of the lost village and station are ½ km west on Dufferin Road 17.

Another near ghost town is the next station village, Corbetton. A string of older homes line the road near the vacant station site, while a church and one-time hotel sit boarded up. A feed elevator stood until the late 1980s.

Dundalk, the next station stop, grew into a busy farming town and stopping place located originally at the Garafraxa Road. However, when the TGB railway builders arrived, they found land prices near the intersection to be too high, and located the station 2 km west. The village followed, and grew into a major regional shipping point. Today the main part of Dundalk clusters about the former station ground where two feed elevators still straddle the right of way, while murals on downtown buildings, depicting train time at the old station, celebrate the community's railway roots.

From Dundalk follow Highway 10 for 8 ½ km north to Grey County Road 34 which leads west to the site of Proton Station. This is one of those satellite communities which developed around the station and outgrew its parent settlement, Proton, on the old pioneer Garafraxa Road (now Highway 10). The businesses are closed now, but several private homes still cluster the abandoned right of way.

A short distance west of Proton Station, the West Back Line leads north to Saugeen Junction. While no community ever formed here, the site was the junction between the TGB and its branch line to Durham, along which the Priceville station survives as a house 10 km west on Grey Road 4. The junction station, however, consisted only of an outhouse-sized waiting room, and the only other building in the area was the section foreman's house, a small grey building which still stands on the west side of the right of way.

The next community on Highway 10 is the revitalized historic town of Flesherton. Located 8 ½ km north of Proton, it has become popular with skiers from the nearby Beaver Valley. Many of its historic buildings have gained new life as antique shops or galleries, while the historic hotel, where stage coaches stopped during pioneer times, now houses a tea room and real estate office.

The rails of the TGB passed a few kilometres west on Grey Road 4, through a community known as Ceylon. While the hamlet has become largely a rural residential community, a few earlier buildings still survive by the right of way.

From Flesherton, stay on Highway 10 for about 9 km north to Markdale, named for Mark Armstrong who donated the land for the TGB station. Here the right of way and the station grounds lie a short distance west on Grey Road 12. A line of trees and one time warehouse are all that remain at the site. The station was moved away to Irish Lake Road where it sat rotting and neglected until it finally collapsed.

From the small village core in Berkeley, a pioneer stopping place on the Garafraxa Road, a cracked sidewalk still leads to the station grounds.

Holland Centre, the next village, looks much like a ghost town, with the vacant hotel and general store guarding the main intersection in the village. As with the others, however, nothing significant remains at the right of way. Both places shipped considerable amounts of lumber, poles, and farm produce out on the railway. Arnott, about six km past Holland Centre, has nearly vanished, along with any evidence that it ever had a station.

At Chatsworth, the right of way crosses the highway to the site of the station grounds. Chatsworth, however, holds two other claims to fame. During pioneer times it was a busy stopping point at the junction of the Garafraxa and Sydenham Roads. With its hotels and taverns, it

The Markdale station was relocated to a nearby field where it rotted until it collapsed.

played a role which it retained until relatively recent times when it was the nearest place to a bone dry Owen Sound in which one could enjoy an alcoholic beverage. During the peak years of rail operation, the town could count 12 stores, 4 hotels, 4 churches, a foundry, saw mill, shingle mill, and butter making plant.

Chatsworth marks the modern junction of Highways 6 and 10. Located 7 ½ km north of this point, Rockford is now just another one of Owen Sound's sprawling suburban crossroads, a far cry from when its small station was once the site of the railway's busiest livestock yard.

Owen Sound presented the railway with its only engineering problem on the northern portion: how to descend the cliffs of the Niagara Escarpment and reach the waters of Georgian Bay. The solution lay in a small gully a short distance east of town which brought it to the bay a few km north of the town itself. From this point the rails had to double back into town and the docks at 1st Ave E.

The rails and the sidings are gone now. However, the handsome modern international style station has survived. And staring right back at it across the inlet, is the former CN station on the old Stratford and Lake Huron line, now preserved as a maritime museum.

7.

The Lake Erie and Northern: Galt to Port Dover

A relative latecomer, the LEN was conceived in 1910 to run from Galt to Port Dover, in part as an attempt by the CPR to develop a ferry connection to cross Lake Erie. Its route took it through Galt and along the east bank of the Grand River to Paris, where it passed under the tracks of the Grand Trunk. It then proceeded south through Brantford to Waterford, where it crossed the THB and the Canada Southern on a high level bridge. From here it angled southeasterly to Simcoe and then to Port Dover, where it originally used the Grand Trunk station, until permission to do so was withdrawn.

A brick CPR plan station was built at Paris, a CPR western plan station at Mount Pleasant, and at Port Dover, an international plan similar to that in Galt, which the LEN shared with the GRR. At Glen Morris, an old stone house beside the river was pressed into service, while in Brantford a two-level station, with the street entrance above, and the tracks below, was shared with Brantford and Hamilton electric railway. Besides 14 station stops the LEN provided 35 flag stops.

Unlike the hourly service enjoyed by the GRR, LEN trains ran only once every two hours. In 1950, the CPR requested the discontinuance of passenger service. When this was refused, the CP reduced service, and the altered timetable included misleading information and inconvenient connections. Not surprisingly, passenger traffic declined markedly, and abandonment was granted in 1955.

In conformity with CPR policy, most stations were soon removed, only those at Mount Pleasant and Port Dover surviving. The line between Simcoe and Port Dover was abandoned in 1962, that between Brantford and Waterford in 1965. The sections from Galt to

Part of the informational display at the trail access point in Glen Morris, this image depicts one of the last of the LEN cars running along the Grand River.

Brantford, and from Waterford to Simcoe lasted until around 1990 when they too were abandoned.

 All Aboard --

The route starts in Galt. From Main St. turn south onto Water St, Highway 24, to follow the routes of both the LEN and the Grand Valley Railway (please see chapter 9). As you proceed south, you will see on the east side of the road yet another abandoned right of way. This is the former Grand Trunk branch which connected Galt with the one-time railway town of Harrisburg on the Grand Trunk's original western main line (before it was re-routed into Brantford around 1900).

Shortly you will come to a 20-space parking lot which marks the start of the Cambridge to Paris Rail Trail which now occupies the LEN right of way. Here, too, an information kiosk explains the history and the

attractions of the rail-trail. Continue along Highway 24 to CR 14 and turn right.

The trail itself offers a number of views of the river and its valley, although during the summer, foliage obscures much of that view. At 4.6 km (three miles) along the trail, a natural spring will quench the thirst of trail users. At 7 km (4.5 miles) the tall stone walls of the Glen Morris mill lie on the west side of the trail. There is no road access to this picturesque ruin, however, if you are following the route by car, a short trail leads to the mill from CR 14 about 2 km north of Glen Morris, and a like distance south of Highway 24.

Another parking lot and information kiosk is located at the end of Washington St in Glen Morris along with a photo of the fine stone house which once was the Glen Morris station. In addition to the station, there were cattle yards here. Closer to Paris, trail users will be able to see the abutments of the former bridge which once carried the

In Glen Morris, an existing house was converted into a station and served this pretty riverside town. This station too has gone.

The former LEN station in Paris was a solid brick structure, but was demolished when the CPR, which controlled the LEN, had no further use for it.

original main line of the Great Western Railway. This short section of ghost railway leads east as far as Lynden Junction, the site of the Brantford realignment. On the way it passes through the villages of St George, where the abutments of the bridge across the highway can still be seen, and the once vital railway junction village of Harrisburg.

In Paris, the LEN rail-trail passes under the current CN bridge to the former station grounds. Once the site of a single storey brick station, a CP pattern, the grounds are, typically, vacant and overgrown. Only vague rubble marks the station location. A steep laneway from the end of William St in Paris leads to the site of the station.

From Paris, the LEN right of way continues into Brantford, interrupted by a gravel pit, where it links with another rail-trail, one which follows an abandoned Toronto Hamilton and Buffalo Railway right of way east toward Hamilton. Together these trails now form part of the Trans Canada Trail.

Brantford, despite its poor record of heritage conservation, has managed to retain some interesting railway buildings. These include the still active GT station located on West St. With its red tile roof, its tower, and rounded waiting room, it was one of the first stations in Canada designated for protection under the federal Heritage Railway

The LEN's Mount Pleasant station sits preserved beside CR 24.

Station Protection Act. VIA trains on the Toronto-Windsor run call here several times a day.

A second railway station, recently restored, is that built by the THB. A stone and brick building, it is located on Market St. a short distance south of the new casino.

In contrast to the portion north of Brantford, that portion of the LEN running south of Brantford to Waterford, abandoned in 1965, has left scarcely a trace.

Its route through the city is represented now by the Brantford Southern Access Road. From Brantford, the Mount Pleasant Rd, or CR 24, parallels the LEN route to Waterford. While the right of way has largely grown over along most of this section, the former Mount Pleasant station was relocated to the east side of the highway, and still retains its original appearance and colour.

The next prominent feature of the LEN comes at Waterford where the high level bridge carried it across the THB and Canada Southern, and still dominates the landscape. The bridge can be viewed by following the roadbed of the old THB south from Mechanic St, to the water's edge. The station grounds stood at the south end of the bridge and at the west end of Nichol St, where, again, only rubble marks the spot.

The LEN's only surviving station is in Port Dover, its heritage ignored.

Happily, Waterford, too, has preserved its other station, that of the Canada Southern, restored as a community facility and located at the west end of Alice St. The apartment building located behind it formerly served as a railway hotel A new museum in town outlines the area's history.

CR 24 south of Waterford continues to parallel the route crossing the right of way at Bloomsburg. In Simcoe, a short walkway follows the right of way between Wilson Ave and Victoria St, the former location of the Simcoe station. Otherwise Hendry St and Basil Ave, both located east of Highway 24, parallel the roadbed.

While the section between Waterford and Simcoe was abandoned only in 1989, leaving the road bed relatively fresh, that from Simcoe to Port Dover was lifted in 1962 and has left little to see. The route continued straight south from Simcoe, parallel to today's Highway 24, to a point just north of Regional Road 3 where it angled sharply southeast, crossing Highway 6 2 km east of Highway 24, and then heading straight east into Port Dover. It then hugged the river to its most recent station at the end of a short lane leading east of St Patrick St a half block north of Nelson St.

Although it still stands, little altered, the building now serves only as a municipal storage facility, yet another all-too-familiar example of heritage neglect.

Despite such failings, Port Dover, with its long sandy public beach, claims to have the world's largest fresh water fishing fleet. The fresh yellow perch which the fishing boats bring home daily, is served up at the historic Erie Beach Hotel, as well as in the town's other restaurants and seasonal cafés. This lakeside resort is a relaxing and convenient place to spend time after following the often scenic route of the LEN.

 # 8.

The Toronto Hamilton and Buffalo Railway: Aberdeen to Waterford

Its distinctive mauve and yellow locomotives are gone, and its logo has vanished from all but the hardest cement bridges. Yet the Toronto Hamilton and Buffalo Railway lives on in the hearts and the minds of many who live in the city where it was based, Hamilton.

The original concept for the THB was to serve American interests by building a link from Buffalo via Hamilton into Toronto. The line would start from a point on the Michigan Central line at Welland, then run through Hamilton and on to Toronto via running rights along the Grand Trunk. This is ironic as the strategy for the TH and B was to break the GT's monopoly in Hamilton. Another branch would lead West of Hamilton, pass through Brantford, and connect back to the Michigan Central at Waterford.

No fewer than four existing railway companies had their fingers in the TH and B pie from the start. These were the New York Central, the Michigan Central, the Canada Southern and the Canadian Pacific, the latter with a 27% interest. Whereas the two American-controlled lines, the MC and the CS, cut across southern Ontario from Buffalo to Detroit, neither had access to the large urban markets at Toronto or Hamilton. The TH and B would provide them that access. In the peninsular part of Niagara, the TH and B thus became the shortest route between Toronto and Buffalo. Today that section remains in use.

West of Hamilton, however, the TH and B has become a ghost railway.

It was here, in 1892, that the TH and B purchased the existing route of Brantford Waterloo and Lake Erie Railway built in 1885 to link Brantford and Waterford. Three years later the line was extended into Hamilton.

A THB locomotive, parked at St. Thomas.

From the TH and B's main facility at the Aberdeen yard, the trains would rumble westward over a trestle across Binkley Hollow. They then faced a 1.5% grade up through the forested hills of Dundas Valley to the aptly named "Summit" where a small shelter was erected. The tracks then emerged onto gently rolling farmlands on their way to Jerseyville. The station here was a Michigan Central style wooden combination depot, with operator's bay, waiting room, and freight shed.

After passing over more bridges, and then under the Grand Trunk's line near Cainsville, the trains entered Brantford where a beautiful station of brick and stone awaited the passengers. After taking on water at the Brantford station, the engines would puff out, crossing the Grand River, and through more rolling farm lands to Scotland.

Between Scotland and Waterford, passengers would gaze upon rolling fields, with occasional glimpses of houses, churches and schools built of the distinctive local fieldstone. At the west end of Waterford, the trains crossed the Waterford ponds, passing beneath the high steel trestle of the Lake Erie and Northern Railway (which the CP also controlled) and easing up to the simple frame Michigan Central station on the old route of the Canada Southern Railway.

Unlike the eight passenger trains which plied the peninsula each day, only two daily passenger trains called along the western section.

In addition to a few farm products and passengers which came on board at the little country stops, the main revenue for this section of the THB was derived from the industries in and around Brantford, such as York Farms Ltd, White Farm Equipment, and Massey Ferguson, and in Scotland where a CIL plant and a lumber yard added to the business.

As roads improved and car travel became the norm, passenger service on this section ended in 1960. Freight service lasted until 1989 when the route was abandoned. It wasn't entirely for lack of business that the end came. Rather, it was a land slippage along a section of fill beside the Grand River. In fact, TH and B tracks remain down in Brantford where trains still serve the local industries. However the shipments now leave town on CN tracks.

 **All Aboard**

Although they remain in use, the historic Aberdeen Yards mark the starting point for this ghost railway. Unfortunately, the historic roundhouse and most other yard buildings have been removed. However, the single storey brick station, its green paint fading, still stood at the time of writing. The yards are located in west end Hamilton on Studholme Road south of Aberdeen Rd.

To continue along the route, take Aberdeen east to Dundurn St and follow it north to Main where you turn left. Follow Main St west to Ostler Dr and turn right (it is Highway 8 all along this section) and follow Ostler Dr.to Governor's Road. Turn left onto Governor's Road, and then left again onto Old Ancaster Road. This will lead you to the abandoned right of way, which at this point is part of the Hamilton Brantford Rail Trail. The 32-km trail links in turn with the SC Johnson Rail Trail in Brantford, and the Grand River trail to make for one nearly continuous rail trail. All these pathways are incorporated into the Trans Canada Trail.

To access the trail, however, you will need to return to Governor's Road and follow it west to the Dundas Valley Conservation Area. Here the trail centre is located in what appears to be an old railway station.

This replica station serves as the centre for the Hamilton Brantford Rail Trail which follows the THB corridor.

But appearances can be deceiving. The building, although styled after the Grand Trunk station in Grimsby (destroyed by fire), it was in fact built only in 1975, and by the conservation authority.

It had been the authority's original intent to operate a tourist train along the then about-to-be abandoned CP track. However, after the wash out, the CP removed the rails, and the dreams of the tourist train died. The beauty of the land through which this section of the trail passes, however, more than compensates for this loss.

Several side trails lead from the rail trail including one to the strange historic ruin known as the Hermitage. Familiar to local trail users, the Hermitage is the ruin of a baronial mansion built in 1855 by George Leith. Gutted by fire in 1934, the walls have been stabilized and make for a startling sight in the lush forests of the valley.

If you are following this line by car, rather than using the trail, return to Governor's Road, and follow it west to Sulphur Springs Rd where you turn south. Here you pass through some of the more scenic sections of this route, as the road, and the trail, wind through steep forested gullies. At Mineral Springs Road turn right and follow the road as it crosses the trail twice in the wooded gully where the hamlet of Mineral Springs is nestled.

This simple wooden shelter served as the Summit station and marked the height of land above the steep grades of the Dundas Valley.

With the roads closed off west of Mineral Springs, you must turn north on Skite Rd and travel to RR 99 which you follow west into Copeland where you turn south onto RR 52. Trail users will pass the site of the former station stop at Summit as well as the Summit Muskeg Conservation Area. Drivers will turn west onto the Jerseyville Road into Jerseyville. Once a busy little farm town, Jerseyville has become a dormitory community for Hamilton and Brantford.

West of the village intersection, you can still trace the old sidewalk which once led to the site of the Jerseyville station. That building survives today in the Westfield Heritage Centre on Highway 8 northwest of Hamilton near the community of Rockton. Jerseyville also offers a parking area and access to the rail trail.

As the trail enters Brantford, it passes beneath the former Highway 2 and then under the tracks of the Grand Trunk before ending at a parking lot on Greenwich St. Drivers will proceed from Jerseyville on RR 217 and 17 before arriving at Highway 2/53. Turn right and follow

Brantford's THB station is not only the most attractive on this route, but one of the nicest in Ontario.

this route which becomes Colborne St upon entering Brantford.

As you travel south on Lock St from Colborne St you can see one of the few surviving sections of the old Grand River Canal, a waterway which linked Brantford with Lake Erie from the 1830s until the 1890s. Lock St leads to Mohawk St which in turn becomes Greenwich St.

In Brantford, some of the old THB track remains in place to serve local industries. But to see the most attractive station on this route, stay on Greenwich St west to Ring Road. Turn left and then left again onto Market St. The beautiful stone and brick station, recently renovated, is on the left at the railway crossing.

Brantford and area offer up some of Ontario's most significant First Nations historic features. On Mohawk St you will find the Royal Chapel of the Mohawks, the newly opened Kanata heritage village, a replica of a Mohawk village, and the world renowned Woodlands Cultural Centre. The birth place of Pauline Johnson, one of Canada's pre-eminent poets, stands a short distance away near the hamlet of Onondaga. Close by is the Alexander Graham Bell homestead where the prolific inventor worked to perfect his telephone, and the location from which he made the world's first long distance phone call, to Paris (Ontario).

To continue on your route follow Market St from the station to

Stark and simple, the THB's station at Waterford was shared with the Michigan Central.

Brantford Southern Access Road (which lies on the old road bed of the LEN - see chapter 7). Turn left onto Mount Pleasant Road, CR 24, where you will pass the relocated station of the LEN. At CR 4, turn right, passing through Oakland to Scotland Station where the THB right of way crosses. The main village of Scotland lies a bit further west, just across Highway 24.

Turn left onto Highway 24. The right of way parallels this road a short distance east. However, there is little to see other than the vacant road bed. To reach Waterford, continue south on Highway 24 to the 8th Concession, or Mechanic St, which leads east into the village.

The right of way crosses Mechanic St. a short distance past the entrance to the Waterford Ponds conservation area. There is a small parking area on the east shore of the ponds. From this parking lot you can walk the right of way to within sight of the high level bridge where the THB passed beneath the tracks of the LEN.

A pretty little farm village with several early buildings, Waterford contains the last of the stations you will see on this line, the old frame ex-Michigan Central station. It sits at the west end of Alice St, the village's main street, and typifies the almost ultra-simple station styles so common south of the border.

9.

The Railways of the Grand River Valley: Berlin to Brantford

The uninitiated may be forgiven for becoming confused over the spaghetti-like pattern of railways which crisscrossed the Grand River valley between Berlin (renamed Kitchener during the first world war) and Brantford, and even beyond. Here were lines like the Grand River, the Grand Valley and the Grand Trunk Railways, along with the Galt and Berlin, and the CPR affiliates, the Toronto Hamilton and Buffalo and the Lake Erie and Northern railways, both of which warrant their own chapters.

The lines snaked up and down both sides of the Grand River valley, crossing and joining in several locations. Even the dedicated rail buff occasionally confuses the various rights of way. Most of these routes have been abandoned, the fate of their road beds ranging from parking lots to hiking trails.

The Grand River Railway

It began as one of Canada's first electric street railways, four miles of track known as the Galt and Preston Street Railway. In 1894, it was built from the Grand Trunk station in Galt, following King and Main to the Speed River in Preston, and the collection of resort hotels known as Preston Springs. The early years were good ones, and by 1896 the line had expanded to Hespeler, newly renamed as the Galt Preston and Hespeler Railway. By 1898 it was carrying 35,000 passengers and 1,000 tons of freight each month, thanks largely to connections with the CPR station at Samuelson St in Galt.

In the meantime, the Preston and Berlin Railway was building from the GPH at East Preston, following a route which took it through Freeport, Centreville, and along King St in Berlin to its junction with

The GRR's Queen St station in Kitchener is shown on an information board near its original site at the start of the Iron Horse Trail, where only the name board has survived.

the Waterloo and Berlin Railway at Albert St. Its Waterloo terminus was at Erb St near the site of today's Waterloo and St Jacob's tourist railway.

Service on the PBR began in 1904 and four years later the line merged with the GPH itself. Car barns and a station were built at Preston Junction, on the north side of the Speed River near the entrance to today's Riverside park. Another station was built at the popular Ildewylde Park, and a terminus added on Guelph St in Hespeler. Later, in 1918, the entire line was renamed the Grand River Railway.

In 1921 the route was realigned through Kitchener between the city limit and Courtland St. To accommodate this new alignment a station was built at Queen St, a wooden structure which was replaced by an attractive Tudoresque brick station in 1943. In Galt, a solid brick station built in the CPR's "international" flat roofed style was added at Main St

Although bus service began in 1925, rail passenger service remained largely uninterrupted until 1938 when it was cut back from Waterloo to the Queen St station in Kitchener. And then following the war, a new passenger coach, the first interurban built in Canada since 1930, was put into service between Kitchener and Galt.

Freight business continued as well, feeding the CPR line in Galt. But the post war auto boom soon began to take its toll and passenger traffic declined, finally ending completely in 1955. The old GRR track was cut back from Centreville to Ottawa St, while a new link was built from a point south of Centreville to a CN spur on the west side of Kitchener. Then, in the 1990's more trackage was removed from between Ottawa St and Victoria Park. Trains continue to use the GRR tracks between Centreville and Preston Junction where a new spur line was built to serve a car assembly plant.

The "Dutch Mill" Line

More properly known as the Galt and Berlin Railway, this line was the Grand Trunk's link from the west side of the Grand River in Galt to the GT main line in Berlin. From a house-like stone station in Galt it followed the west bank of the Grand River, passing through the little mill towns of Blair and Doon before heading inland and through the west side of Berlin. Passenger service was discontinued in 1932, and the line from Galt to the south side of Kitchener was abandoned in 1964.

This unlikely looking structure was the Grand Trunk's Galt station for the GBR.

The Grand Valley Railway

The GVR traces its origins back to the 1870s with the incorporation of the Brantford Street Railway. A strictly local line, the BSR was built in 1886 and electrified in 1892. Then, in 1902, the line acquired the charter of the Port Dover Brantford Berlin and Goderich Railway (another of those pie in the sky names) and began building north towards Paris. In 1904 the route reached Galt via the river road on the east side of the Grand, and was renamed the Grand Valley Railway.

However, the Galt portion was a constant money loser, and was cut back to Paris in 1916. In 1919 a new station was built in Paris, but the line was abandoned ten years later when buses replaced the radial coaches.

 All Aboard _____

This route follows the abandoned portions of the various Grand River lines from Kitchener to Brantford. The route begins in Victoria Park in downtown Kitchener, near the former yards of the Grand River

Railway. While housing dominates the site of the St Joseph St yards, the right of way is evident at the north end of the park near Park St.

Follow Park St south through these historic grounds to Queen St and go west to the sign for the Iron Horse Trail. Here, at the site of the former GRR station, an information plaque outlines the history of the railway and marks the access to the trail. The trail follows the former roadbed south, crossing Courtland St and ending near Ottawa St. Beyond that the old right of way is occupied respectively by Delta St and then King St which is now a four-lane thoroughfare.

Although a few rail era buildings mark the once distinct hamlet of Centreville, just north east of the intersection of King and Fairway, the old right of way has vanished. On the south side of Fairway Road, where the new CN line swings in from the west, you can still see a portion of the original alignment. From here into Preston the line remains in use as an industrial spur.

Preston retains a number of interesting railway vestiges. Although the historic shops were levelled within the last decade (for no discernable reason), the last section of line into Hespeler is now a short rail trail. You can access the trail at the end of Russ St in Preston and follow the original route of the Preston and Hespeler Street Railway (the tracks were moved when flooding became a problem.) The trail passes the site of the former Speedsville station which served the once busy mill town and was home of the Speedsville Woolen Mill whose ruins remain visible on the north side of the trail. The trail then passes under Highway 401 and through the site of Idylwild Park, a playground popular with railway excursionists until it closed in 1916. The trail leaves the roadbed at Beaverdale, the site of another station. In Hespeler the last GRR station was demolished in the mid-1990s to expand a parking lot.

Another legacy of the GRR's heyday is the large and historic Del Monte Hotel, now being converted to a retirement home, which still dominates the busy intersection of Fountain and King Sts.

From Preston follow the 401 west to exit 275. Take Homer Watson Blvd. north to Conestoga College Blvd and Doon Valley Dr. Then drive west to Pinnacle Dr which leads northeast into the former mill town of Doon. Here the right of way of the Galt and Berlin Railway crosses, still visible, while on Old Mill Dr, the stone foundations of Doon's historic

A portion of the Galt and Berlin railway is now a short hiking trail. This point of entry is in the historic mill town of Blair.

mill stand beside the creek.

Return to Homer Watson Blvd, and go south, crossing the 401 to where Homer Watson becomes Fountain St. After a short distance turn right onto Blair Rd. Look immediately on the west side of the road. Here the embankment of the GBR is quite visible, as is a small stone bridge over a brook.

Blair itself is a treasure trove of heritage buildings, the most important of which are Lamb's Inn, built in 1837, and, just west on Mill St, the peculiar sheave tower, recently restored. Opposite the inn a small parking lot marks the trail which follows the GBR, and contains an informational sign which describes the railway and other historic features of the vicinity. Leave the parking lot, following Blair Rd into Galt, where you turn right onto George St. At the north east corner of George and Gardiner, a small stone house, now an office, is the unlikely looking former Grand Trunk station for the GBR.

Cross the Grand River into Galt using Main St. Here the historic downtown has been nicely restored, as have a number of the old stone mills along the banks of the river. From Main St turn south onto Water St, Highway 24. To follow the route of the GVR turn from Highway 24 right onto CR 14 which hugs the valley of the Grand. The Cambridge to Paris Rail Trail which was built along the route of the LEN also parallels this road and is outlined in Chapter 7.

While most of the Grand Valley Railway has been obscured by CR 14, a few remnants remain visible. Just north of Paris, the road bed and the ruins of a generating station which powered the GVR can be seen from the LEN rail trail. These lie a short distance north of the GTR's abandoned main line, and its bridge abutments by the Grand River.

In Paris, the GVR entered town at a lower level than that of the LEN, following CR 14 as it becomes Willow St. Here, on the east side,

Of the four railway stations which once stood in Paris, only that of the G.V.R. survived. Today it is a pretty private home.

at the corner of Brant St, is the Paris station for the GVR. Now a house, and partially obscured by shrubbery, it still retains its distinctive bay window.

Paris is mentioned in the chapter on the Buffalo Brantford and Huron Railway. But it is worth repeating here as well. Attractively situated in the steep valley of the Grand, Paris has retained its charming main street, and many of its handsome homes, several of which are built of cobblestone, a construction technique peculiar to Paris. Because of the proliferation of gypsum in the banks of the Grand River in this vicinity, the town has lent its name to the world renowned sculpting material, plaster of Paris.

An aspect of its history that is less well known is that Paris was a key railway town, having once been the focus of four different railway lines. That history is behind it now, as only one line, that of the CNR, passes through town, and the train doesn't stop here any more.

From Paris you can link up with the continuation of the LEN rail trail which continues southward into Brantford.

10.

The Buffalo Brantford and Goderich: Fort Erie to Stratford

The 1850s were rife with speculation over where Ontario's rail lines were going to go, or not go. As the Grand Trunk and Great Western Railways began to establish the routes of their trunk lines, towns and villages clamoured to be on them. But, despite the eagerness of the municipalities to welcome the railway, land owners held out for top dollar, forcing the railway to give many of them a wide berth. And this was no less the case with the merchants of Brantford.

Weary of shipping their products and importing their raw materials along the slow and seasonal Grand River Canal, they demanded fast year-round access which only the railways could provide. In 1849, when the Great Western was surveying a route which would pass to the north of Brantford, the group formed a company to raise money for a railway which would link Buffalo with Goderich on Lake Huron. To their delight their initiative met with favour both in Buffalo and with municipalities along the proposed route.

Surveys began, commencing in Fort Erie, then west to the Grand River where the surveyors followed the east bank into Brantford. The line then crossed the Grand at Paris before angling northwesterly to Stratford.

In Stratford it met a roadblock in the form of John Gwynn. Gwynn was trying to promote another railway, one which would run from Toronto to Guelph and on to Goderich, and worked to lobby parliament to deny the BBG permission to proceed beyond Stratford. Gwynn failed, and the legislature approved the "Buffalo Brantford and Goderich Railway". There were, however, no government funds. In fact the BBG was the only railway in its day to be built without government subsidy.

Finally, in 1854, even before the Grand Trunk had opened its Montreal to Toronto line, the first wood burning steam engine puffed into Brantford from Buffalo. As the local newspaper noted, it was "a grand gala day to the inhabitants of this town and the surrounding country. At 8 o'clock there was a general display of fireworks in front of the court house. The Grand Railway Ball took place in the second storey of the depot machine shops which were tastefully decorated. Not less than 1500 persons were present, most of whom tripped the light fantastic until broad daylight. There were two bands of musicians present, one a cotillion band from Buffalo, and the other the Brantford Philharmonic."

But the railway's problems were not over. Two months later, the joy turned to rage when the railway buildings were set ablaze and destroyed. Then, when the rails reached Stratford in September, it came face to face with the Grand Trunk which unceremoniously removed the BBG's rails. The BBG boss then ordered his local contractor to "tear up the Grand Trunk and re-lay the BBG, and set men to watch it." But the GT had plans of its own, and sent in two car loads of armed and drunken navies. However, wiser heads prevailed and the confrontation was avoided.

Not so in Ridgeway. Later the same year, angry at not being paid in full, 30 BBG labourers began to rip up the tracks. The BBG then began to re-lay using "scab" workers guarded by 25 special constables. In the fight which followed, one man was killed, and several injured.

Finally, in 1858, the line reached Goderich and instantly hit the profit column. With a new terminus at Goderich, lake freighters were now able to make two trips a year instead of just one, while townsfolk along the line eagerly rode the rails to enjoy the cool breezes of the lake in the hot summers, a treat few had previously experienced.

At Fort Erie, a ferry shuttled across the entrance to the Niagara River from Buffalo to a wharf terminal near the walls of old Fort Erie. The Fort Erie terminal was relocated into the old downtown area, and then later to the Grand Trunk's new station in Victoria, later renamed Bridgeburg (today it is part of Fort Erie itself).

From Fort Erie the line then ran straight across country to meet the Welland Railway at Port Colborne, where the first station stood at the diamond between the two lines on the east side of the canal, rather than on the west side as the present station does today. By now the line had been renamed the Buffalo and Lake Huron, before being absorbed by the GT in 1869.

With the building of the railway, Buffalonians began to eye the clean sandy beaches of Lake Erie, and a number of amusement parks and cottage colonies, primarily American, began to take over the shoreline. The park at Crystal Beach, which began as a religious colony, soon had its own railway, the Ontario Southern Railway, which connected with the BBG at Ridgeway. Nicknamed the "Peg Leg," its track consisted of a single T- shaped rail set on posts.

Closer to Fort Erie was the Fort Erie Beach Amusement park. It, too, enjoyed a railway between 1885 and 1910. Known as the Fort Erie Snake Hill and Pacific, its tracks followed the shore of the lake from the original steamer landing beside the fort to the beach a short distance away.

In addition to the parks, there appeared more prestigious cottage colonies. Solid Comfort, west of Port Colborne, was the exclusive enclave of the U.S.-based Humberstone Summer Resort Company, and had the use of its own flag station on the line. The street name of Tennessee Avenue in today's Port Colborne carries the legacy of this one time American colony.

Meanwhile, east of Port Colborne, a flag station named Lorraine served yet another American outpost from which many of the residents commuted to work in Buffalo. American dominance of Ontario's Lake Erie shore has not yet ended. The private American-dominated enclave at Point Abino still refuses non-residents access along their private road to the remarkable lighthouse at the point, even though the lighthouse has recently been designated as a Canadian National Historic Site.

West of Port Colborne, the BBG established a station at Wainfleet, where the GT later built one of its few conical roof stations, likely because the site was popular with tourists. A short distance beyond, again near a busy beach, it located a small flag station called Lowbanks.

As it approached the Grand River, it swung to the northwest and into Dunnville. Thanks to the traffic on the Grand River Canal, Dunnville was already well established as a river port, with a market

An attractive BBG station was built by the Grand Trunk in Dunnville. It was replaced by a smaller and simpler structure which was relocated before being destroyed by fire.

area and commercial core close to the river. This forced the railway to establish its station grounds away from the built-up area and well inland from the river. Ironically, it was the arrival of the BBG that eventually killed most of the traffic on the Grand River canal.

The GT's Dunnville station was an attractive building with towers by both the tracks and the entrance.

From this point the line cut across country, crossing the Canada Southern and the Canada Air Line at Canfield Junction. There were small stations to serve York, named Seneca station, and Indiana, where a sawmill village named Cooks Station grew by the tracks. With the death of the Grand River canal, Indiana vanished, becoming a ghost town, a fate which likewise befell Cooks Station when the sawmill ended operation.

Caledonia was both a river town and key stopping place on the vital Hamilton to Port Dover road. Because the town was already well built up on the banks of the river, the BBG was again forced to locate its station grounds away from the water. North of Caledonia, small stations were located at Middleport, Onondaga, Cainsville and then finally at Brantford, near where the current VIA station stands.

At Paris, the tracks crossed the Grand River on a high level bridge

CN's attractive Bridgeburg station in Fort Erie was demolished when CN had no further use for it.

before meeting the Great Western main line. Here, at Paris Junction, a sizeable village grew up, and was eventually connected to the main part of the town, when the town's growth moved in that direction.

From Paris, the route carried the line across Ontario's fertile farmlands, finally entering Stratford, where it shared a station with the GT at the corner of Guelph and Downie Streets.

 ## All Aboard

Not all of the BBG is abandoned, at least not yet. Short line operations still shine the rails between Brantford and Caledonia, and between Goderich and Stratford. The short section of the old line between Paris and Brantford has become part of the busy CN main line between Windsor and Toronto, carrying eight VIA trains each day.

The route begins in that section of Fort Erie once known as Bridgeburg, or Victoria. Now called Fort Erie North, it was once a busy railway town. Here, once a bridge was built, the tracks of the BBG, the Canada Southern and the Canada Air Line all merged to cross the Niagara River. Railway stations were built on both the north and south sides of the track, that of the Michigan Central on the north, and the GT on the south. Despite the demise of the BGG and the Canada Southern, the bridge remains busy carrying both CN and CP trains across the river to Buffalo.

Courtright St on the north side of the tracks was once lined with railway hotels, while the crew bunkhouse stood on Lewis St. on the south side. Jarvis St., meanwhile, developed as the "main drag", a role which it plays to this day, although it is quieter now thanks to competition from the large malls at Niagara Falls.

The GT station was one of Ontario's most attractive, with its "witch's hat" conical roof rising above the waiting room. While it has gone, the old Michigan Central station, which later took over the Canada Southern, was moved a short distance away to the Fort Erie Railroad Museum on Central Avenue. Also at the museum, you will find a steam locomotive, and the former GT station relocated from Ridgeway.

Follow Central Ave south to Bertie St and take it east to the river. Here, on Niagara Blvd stood the old station of the Erie and Niagara Railway (later part of the Canada Southern) until 1997. It served as a shop until it was replaced with a newer building. Follow Niagara Blvd south as it becomes Lakeshore Rd and leads to one of Ontario's most historic attractions, old Fort Erie. At this point Dominion Rd becomes the main route, while Lakeshore Rd veers south of the fort to the site of Fort Erie Beach park. Dominion Rd continues west as CR 1 with the abandoned right of way paralleling it a short distance to the south.

At Ridge Rd. turn south to enter the old downtown portion of Ridgeway. Here, a number of early buildings yet date from the days of rail, including an early railway hotel. To reach the village of Crystal Beach, and the condominiums which have now replaced the amusement park, follow Farr Ave west from Ridge Rd to Ridgeway Rd which leads south to Erie Rd and the now nearly ghosted downtown part of Crystal Beach.

Then, from Erie Rd take Derby Rd north through the historic residential section of the village, where the streets radiate out from a central park. Derby Rd ends at Michener Rd, CR 1, where you turn left. Then, when you come to CR 112, Abino Road, turn right to get to Highway 3 (unless you want to go south to Point Abino and argue with a security guard over access to the lighthouse).

Follow Highway 3 west as it passes close to the village of Sherkston where a small flag station stood across from the old general store. Continue on Highway 3 to RR 5, Killaly St, which you follow into the eastern end of Port Colborne. This takes you to Welland St. where you turn left to find "old" Port Colborne. Here the right of way lies between Fraser St and Durham, the location of Port Colborne's first station and its original commercial core. When the station relocated to the west side of the canal, so, too, did the businesses. Today, "old" Port Colborne almost resembles a ghost town, while the "new" town remains busy.

While the old right of way is abandoned, a new spur from the north curves in front of the station, and follows the BBG a short distance west to the site of a cement plant. The station, while retaining its exterior appearance, has a new tenant, Joe Fetas' Greek Restaurant. Several blocks to the west the former Port Colborne yards lie weedy and overgrown.

The parks by the Welland Canal in Port Colborne offer excellent vantage points from which to watch the mighty ocean freighters glide under the lift bridge and into Lake Erie.

To find the once exclusive Solid Comfort enclave, follow King St south to Sugarloaf St. A short distance west, Tennessee Ave, the site of this one-time American colony, winds its way along the shore of the lake.

To exit Port Colborne, follow Lakeshore Rd west from Tennessee Ave to Augustine Rd and turn south. Just after the bend in the road, look to your right to see the little conical- roofed station which once sat at Wainfleet. Little altered, it is now a private home. To reach the site of the station grounds, return up Augustine Rd to Highway 3 and follow that route west to where it bends north and RR 3 continues straight ahead. Stay on RR 3 and follow it as it bends south. "W Station Rd" marks the location of the old grounds. No structures stand here now.

Continue west along RR 3 which follows the lakeshore, and the many new homes built there, to RR 65 and the early summer resort of Lowbanks. Follow RR 65 north where after a km you cross the abandoned right of way, and the site of the little flag station. Then, turn left at Highway 3 to Dunnville.

Entering the town, look on the left for Lehman's car dealership. This simple modern looking building formerly served as the station for the Port Maitland branch of the Toronto Hamilton and Buffalo Railway. Maple St, which crosses Highway 3, leads west to the old portion of the canal-side town, at Market and Front St. where a handful of early buildings have managed to survive the onslaught of parking lots and fast food chains.

Maple St also leads east to Cayuga St and the now overgrown site of the station grounds. The sad spectacle is now marked with rubble, non-descript small industries, and vacant factories. The only legacy of the railway era is the Savoy Hotel, a modest tavern that was once a railway hotel.

Dunnville still boasts an attractive and busy downtown area, as well as two riverside parks. If you want a side trip to old Port Maitland, take RR 3, Dover Rd, across the bridge, to Port Maitland Road which leads the six km to this tranquil lakeside oasis.

Otherwise, continue west on Highway 3 and branch left onto CR 17, to follow the river. After approximately four km, turn right onto Junction Road which leads north to the former railway junction point of Canfield Junction. While no railway structures survive at the site of the diamond, a few workers' homes line the road. At this writing, there are still rails on both the CS and the Air Line, but appearances suggest they won't be there much longer.

Here you again meet Highway 3 which leads west into Canfield village where a one time feed mill still stands by the right of way. Continue on Highway 3 into Cayuga, an early canal town with several historic buildings, including the former county court building. In Cayuga turn north onto RR 54 and follow the river to the historic canal town of York. Along the way take time to visit the national historic site of Ruthven, a mansion built by a local industrialist and former politician named David Thompson.

This stately pillared home, now open to the public (sorry, summers only) also marks the site of the ghost town of Indiana. This town once held 300 residents and could boast 30 industries. Today only a pair of homes and a badly overgrown graveyard remain to mark the spot.

North of York, the road continues along the river and into the town of Caledonia, a place worth visiting. Here, Argyle St crosses the Grand

River on a 9-span concrete arch bridge on the east end of which a red brick house once housed the village toll keeper. On the west side of the bridge you can visit the now restored Caledonia mills.

And for rail lovers, there's the station.

Besides being between two lock stations on the Grand River Canal, Caledonia was also the junction of two railway lines, the BBG and the Hamilton and Northwestern. When the GT realigned the crossing in 1913, the old station was removed and a new one built. After passenger service ended in 1957, and express parcel service two decades after that, CN allowed the station to fall into disrepair, threatening in 1996 to tear it down. However, led by Ron Clark, local residents rallied to save the building. Now returned to its original GT colours, it serves as a museum. You will find it just west of the railway crossing on Argyle St.

And the trains still stop here. Today a short line out of Hamilton still provides service to local industries via Brantford.

You can leave Caledonia by following Highway 54 is it follows the bank of the Grand River to CR 18. Follow CR 18 west until you come to CR 4 and turn right. This becomes Erie Ave and enters Brantford from the south. At the corner of Erie and Market Sts you will see on the right the attractive stone and brick station built by the THB (see Chapter 8) Brantford's magnificent GT station sits on West St on the south side of the tracks. Designated as a heritage station by the federal government, it still sees several trains a day, passenger and freight.

Between Brantford and Paris, the old BBG line is as busy as any line in Ontario, being the main CN line between Toronto and Windsor.

Follow Highway 2 from Brantford to Paris, the once busy junction of the BBG and the GW. Because it followed higher ground, the BBG built its line along a bluff overlooking the main part of Paris, which lay by the river. Here the GW arrived from the east having laid its Toronto main line, much to Brantford's annoyance, further north through Harrisburg.

It took until the turn of the century before Brantford could persuade the GT, the GW's new owner, to re-route its line south from Harrisburg through Brantford, and then back up along the old route of the BBG to Paris. After doing so, the GT abandoned the Harrisburg to Paris portion. You can still see this abandoned right of way today as it angles across Grand River Rd between Golf Links Rd and the retirement home. Golf Links Rd will also lead you to the bridge abutments which mark the original GW bridge over the Grand River.

To reach the site of Paris Junction follow Broadway St W to Spruce St just over the crossing. This was the site of the first station, and where the old right of way of the BBG leads northwesterly from the current main line. Paris's second station stood near Broadway St E, but it too has been removed.

To leave Paris, drive north from Spruce St to Silver St and proceed west. Silver St eventually becomes CR 36 ending at a T-intersection with Trussler Rd. Turn right here and travel to the third road on your left, Township Road 5, and follow it about 4.5 km to Richwood. Here you can observe the depression in the ground where the right of way once passed beneath the road.

From Richwood continue west to CR 3 and follow it north to Drumbo. Drumbo grew from a crossroads hamlet to become a railway junction when, in quick succession, it welcomed the BBG and the Credit Valley Railway (now the CP). The station grounds of the BBG are now a storage yard on the west side of CR 3 just north of the village's main intersection. While the station has long vanished, the former station hotel, a red brick building, sits on the south side of the road, opposite the station grounds.

Return to the main intersection in Drumbo and follow CR 29 west to CR 22, which leads north to Bright, the next station stop. The right of way crosses the road two blocks before the stop sign for CR 8. While new housing has obliterated the route on the left, a small industry, once a warehouse, still occupies its original rail side location on the right. Just beyond it, also on the right, sits the post office and former railway hotel.

From Bright follow CR 8 west to Blandford Road and turn right. Continue through the crossroads hamlet of Ratho for another ½ km to where the road jogs, and where the failed rail town of the same name lies.

Ratho contains one of those landscape incongruities which vestige seekers relish. When the rails of the BBG appeared on the horizon, Ratho was laid out as a sizable town in anticipation of becoming a place of some importance. But the prosperity never arrived, and Ratho remained a country station. However, the evidence of early confidence lies in the large hotel and store, a handsome red brick structure, which still retains its porch, yet appears strangely out of place surrounded by farmland. The jog in the road represents the efforts to develop a street pattern, streets that were either never constructed or which have vanished.

Then return to CR 3 and continue west to CR 59 and follow it north into Tavistock. Here, at Tavistock, the rails of the Stratford and Port Dover Railway, lifted before the turn of the century, bent southward (please refer to *Ghost Railways of Ontario: Volume One*). The rails of the BBG however continued straight through the community. The right of way is still evident north of the intersection of CR 59 and CR 24, where, on the left, an old freight shed still stands, and where the station platform is still evident. The station itself was moved to Jacob St where it has been altered to become a private residence.

The last leg of the route leads to Stratford. From Tavistock continue north on CR 107 to Highway 7/8, and the aptly named hamlet of Shakespeare, and turn right.

Before gaining fame for its Shakespearean festival, Stratford was one of Ontario's premier railway towns. After the GT had finished its many amalgamations it began to search for a location suitable for repair shops. Stratford's midwestern location proved ideal, and the town became a busy railway centre. In addition to the shops, there was a large railway YMCA, and to supply plants and shrubs to beautify the various station grounds, a large greenhouse.

Today, the many railway lines that once stabbed into southwestern Ontario's country side have been halved, the shops, greenhouses and original Y gone. The vast yards today store only a small fleet of engines operated by Rail Tex on its Goderich and Exeter line. Much less busy now, the handsome stone station, built in 1913, sees only four passengers trains a day.

While Stratford marks the end of this route, it is also the starting point for your pursuit of the Stratford and Huron Railway (see Chapter 4), or the Lake Huron and Port Dover, (please see *Ghost Railways of Ontario: Volume One*). It is also a good place to pause and enjoy the ambience of the park system along the Avon River, and the preserved buildings of the historic downtown, do some train spotting, and then take in a show.

11.

The Cataract Lines: Hamilton's Lost Electric Railways

Despite being Ontario's second largest city, Hamilton remains, undeservedly so, something of a heritage backwater. With multi-cultural Toronto at one end of the QEW, and the high profile attractions of Niagara Falls and Niagara-on-the-Lake near the other, few historical enthusiasts pay Hamilton much heed. Yet the city contains a rejuvenated waterfront, a castle larger than Casa Loma, and two of Canada's most attractive railway stations.

And it was the centre of Canada's most extensive system of radial railways, known locally as the "Cataract." In 1896 the Cataract was first incorporated as the Cataract Power Company to develop hydro-electric power from the cataract at Decew Falls near St Catharines. In 1903 it changed its name to the Hamilton Cataract Power Light and Traction Company, and brought the separately operating radial systems under single control.

In 1907 they built a four-storey terminal building in downtown Hamilton. Located at the southeast corner of Catharine and King the building also served as the main office for the company's network of radial lines, and was considered the only "grand" station in Canada built exclusively for a radial railway. The waiting room on the ground floor measured 20 m by 35 m (68' by 108') with a soaring 6 m (20') ceiling.

From this terminal radial lines stabbed out easterly to Vineland, southwesterly to Brantford, northwesterly to Dundas, and northeasterly to Oakville. And they might have gone further, to Lake Erie, to Toronto, to Niagara, and to Guelph, had other jurisdictions fulfilled their promises, and had the auto age not interfered.

By the 1930s buses and cars had replaced electric railways, and radial lines across Canada closed down. Although when Ontario Hydro sold off the bus route portion of the Hamilton Grimsby and Beamsville line to private interests, it was on the condition that electric railway competition be halted. Streetcars were cut up for scrap, lines were removed, and tracks paved over. Because few of Hamilton's radials operated on private rights of way, or built elaborate stations, little remains to see of this once ubiquitous form of transportation.

With today's road congestion, pollution and truck accidents, it is an era that ended too soon.

The Hamilton and Dundas Street Railway Company: Hamilton to Dundas

One of Canada's oldest street railways was the Hamilton and Dundas. It began service in 1876 using a device known as "dummy" engines. Because many residents objected to the possibility of steam engines puffing along city streets, the operators simply placed small steam locomotives within the shell of a streetcar. This seemed to satisfy everyone for two decades until 1897 when the line was at last electrified.

Its route took it from Hatt and Foundry St in Dundas, along Hatt to Dundas St, and then along Dundas Creek, through Ainslie Woods and on into Hamilton via Aberdeen, Queen, Charlton, Mcnab and Main. At the beginning, it used the GT station located on Ferguson Ave before moving to the new Terminal Station in 1907.

At its peak it could offer service every half hour. However, by 1923, bus competition became too much, and service ended. Some portions of the trackage in Dundas were taken over by the THB, while the Hamilton Street Railway helped itself to other trackage in Hamilton.

The Hamilton Grimsby and Beamsville Electric Railway Company: Hamilton to Vineland

In 1894 when the radials began running between Hamilton and Grimsby, the HGB became Canada's first major electrified radial railway line. In 1896, it was extended to Beamsville where a single stall car house, with waiting room attached, was built. For a few years it operated as far as Vineland, anticipating a further extension right to St Catharines. However, the municipal council in St Catharines refused to build the necessary bridge, and the Vineland extension was scrapped soon after.

A radial car of the HGB crosses the Red Hill embankment east of Hamilton

Many radials carried not just passengers but freight as well. Because of its easy access to the many fruitlands which once existed between Hamilton and Beamsville, both the GT and THB railways made connections with the radial line: the GT was at Winona, the THB at their Kinnear yard in Hamilton. Produce was at first physically transferred from HGB cars to those of the GT or CP. Later, however, the radial cars actually hauled regular freight cars behind them.

From the new downtown terminal, which it began using in 1907, its route took it along Main St to Sherman, then along Maple, Trolley (later Gage) to Lawrence and east on Lawrence to Bartonville. Here it switched to a private right of way to Red Hill, and then back to what is now Regional Road 8 all the way to Beamsville. Station stops were located at Bartonville, Stoney Creek, Fruitland, Smiths (the site of a busy cannery) Winona, Pattisons, Roberts, Grimsby, Grimsby Beach and in the car barn at Beamsville where a small waiting room was placed. Aside from the downtown terminal, most of these "stations"were either small shelters or were placed in an existing building.

Like most radial lines, it became heavily involved in recreational excursions with blossom specials and trips to Grimsby Beach and Grimsby Park.

Then, in 1927, the Cataract began operating buses themselves, and following takeover by the Hydro Electric Power Commission of Ontario in 1931, the bus line was sold and streetcar service ended entirely.

Hamilton Radial Electric Railway: Hamilton to Oakville

The brainchild of one John Patterson, his vision in 1893 was to build a radial network 360 km (227 miles) in extent linking Hamilton with Toronto, Niagara Falls, and even Woodstock. The first rails were laid that year from James St in Hamilton to Hamilton Beach. Then, in 1895 when the hoped-for partner CPR pulled out, the ambitious scheme was radically cut back. In 1898 it was built only to Burlington, and in 1905 to Oakville.

From Hamilton its route carried it along James St. then Gore, Wilson and Sherman, where a private right of way paralleled the road. It then paralleled Barton St to Hamilton Beach where it ran beside the GT entering Burlington on Maple St. From Burlington it ran easterly along Elgin, James and New St to Oakville where New St becomes Rebecca St and then Randall St.

But even in the 1920s some dreams lived on. In an era when buses were quickly replacing streetcars, the HEPC envisioned an electric railway from Toronto to Port Credit, and then linking with the HRE at Oakville. However, the scheme collapsed, and in 1925, the HRE was instead cut back from Oakville to Port Nelson

The HRE's main facilities included a 17-car barn in Burlington and a steam power plant on Burlington Beach. Separate stations stood on Hamilton Beach, in Oakville, and in Burlington. The latter, built in 1927, served as a Hydro office and store following the end of the line, while that in Oakville still survives as a retail establishment. The beach station survived until the 1980s when it was finally removed. The Burlington Beach power house was removed in 1947, and the Burlington car barn, in 1962.

The Brantford and Hamilton Electric Railway Company

Of all Hamilton's interurban lines, this more resembled a regular railway. It ran across country for most of its route, and followed a private of way. Although first proposed in 1896, it did not open until a decade

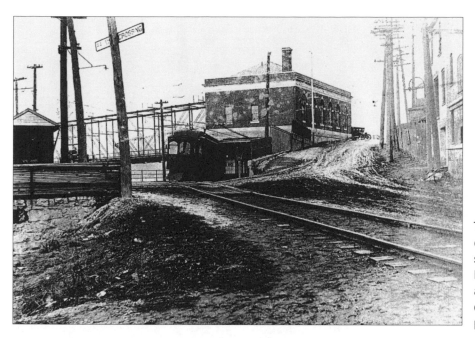

The Brantford station of the HBR was shared with the LEN. Passengers entered at street level and descended to the platform.

later. Its open route allowed for higher rates of speed than most radial cars could manage, and larger cars were built for that reason.

Its route took it from the Terminal Station in downtown Hamilton and then west on Main to Hess where it headed south to near Aberdeen. From Queen and Aberdeen, the tracks began a long ascent up the limestone face of Hamilton Mountain. Halfway up the mountain was Sanatorium Station, past which the line climbed the cliff face, a route followed today by the 403. Views which unfold for drivers today were enjoyed by streetcar passengers eight decades ago. Although then the view was one of fields and forests, not malls and condos.

Along the way there were small stations at James St, Summit, Alberton, Langford, Cainsville and Mohawk Park. The line terminated at a bi-level station built in 1915 by the Lake Erie and Northern in downtown Brantford. In 1925, the line amalgamated with the HRE and ran through trains from Brantford to Burlington.

After the auto age arrived in the early 1920s, the line began to operate at a loss. Following the inauguration of bus service the volume of passenger traffic declined by half. In 1930, the HEPC acquired the assets, selling the bus line, and, as it did with the HBG, closing the electric service so as not to compete with buses. Service ended in 1931.

Top: The former power house for the HGB radial cars is now a popular
restaurant in Stoney Creek.
Above left: The only single-purpose station to survive the era of
Hamilton's electric railways is the one at Oakville.
Above right: The vestiges of the bridge which carried the HER cars across
Bronte Creek may one day be engulfed by the footings for a
new road bridge.

While the stations were demolished, and the rails lifted, some of the rolling stock ended up with Canada Crushed Stone Corporation of Dundas on an electric railway run by that company. The cars were still in use as recently as 1971.

 ## All Aboard

With little in the way of major infrastructure to begin with, the Hamilton radial lines have left little to see. The most significant structure, the Terminal Station, was removed in 1959 to be replaced by the Tower apartments, and is now the site of an office building.

Other stations do survive, however. The office building which housed the Stoney Creek waiting room for the HGB still stands in the downtown part of Stoney Creek, at 32 King St. A block north, the Powerhouse Restaurant now occupies the power house which supplied electrical power to the trains in this area. In Oakville, the attractive little brick building which doubled as a waiting room and substation for the HER remains unchanged on Randall St.

Because they followed the shoulders of roads which have since been paved and widened, few rights of way remain visible. The best example however is that of the HB. It remains distinguishable in several areas south of old Highway 2 between the Copetown Road and Cainsville. While the large bridge that formerly carried the streetcars over Oakville Creek has been replaced with a wider highway bridge, the abutments for the abandoned bridge over Twelve Mile Creek in Bronte can still be seen on Rebecca St where it dead ends west of Bronte Rd. However, a proposal to build a new bridge at this location will likely obliterate these last vestiges of the HER.

12.

The Niagara St Catharines and Toronto Railway: Port Colborne to Port Dalhousie

From the earliest days of European settlement, Ontario's Niagara Peninsula was the focus of a dense network of transportation routes. Construction of the first of four Welland Canals to bypass Niagara Falls began in 1824. Ontario's first "railway", the horse-drawn Erie and Ontario, was constructed as a portage around the Niagara Falls in 1835, and was soon followed by other railways which seemed to be running off in all directions.

The Great Western railway was followed by the Grand Trunk, the Canada Southern, the Canada Air Line and the Toronto Hamilton and Buffalo. While these all served interests beyond the area, one railway was built to serve the area itself, and that was the Niagara St Catharines and Toronto Railway.

After the Grand Trunk and the Great Western amalgamated in 1882, freight rates in the St Catharines area increased noticeably, much to the anger of local politicians. To compete with the monopoly, a number of prominent citizens in St Catharines formed a company which would build a new steam railway. From Niagara Falls in the east, where it would connect with the Michigan Central, it would run westerly through St Catharines to Canfield, and ultimately to a connection with the CPR. It also envisioned branch lines to both Hamilton and Queenston.

Known first as the St Catharines and Niagara Central, it completed a route from Niagara Falls to Thorold in 1887, and to St Catharines in 1888. However, when the THB was built through Smithville and Welland, the SNC's western aspirations were thwarted, and the line fell into disuse.

But it would not long lay dormant. In 1899 the little railway roared

An early view of one the NST's radial cars.

back to life as the Niagara St Catharines and Toronto Railway. It would change from steam to cheaper electric power, and proposed tentacles to Port Colborne, Port Dalhousie and Toronto. One of the first extensions completed was that to Port Dalhousie in 1901. It then went on to acquire a series of local street railways which allowed it to expand throughout the peninsula.

At its peak, the NST extended from its main terminal on St Paul St. in St Catharines to Welland in 1907, Port Weller and Niagara-on-the-Lake in 1913, and Port Colborne in the same year. By 1913, the NST had acquired the Port Dalhousie branch of the Welland Railway, and offered routes into the Lake Ontario port along both sides of the Welland canal.

Rebuffed in its attempts to reach Toronto by rail, for which it blamed the Hamilton radial lines, the NST began steamship service from Port Dalhousie on the steamers Lakeside and Garden City. The NST, as did so many interurban railways, opened up a park in order to attract business on holidays. It was this way, in 1902, that Port Dalhousie acquired present-day Lakeside Park, complete with merry-go-round, midway, and baseball diamond. Steamer service outlasted the NST itself, finally being terminated by the CN in 1950.

One of Ontario's most outstanding railway stations was that of the NST in Niagara Falls. Located near today's Oakes Garden, it lasted a mere 12 years, before being demolished in 1940.

In 1908 the NST was acquired by the interests of railway builders William McKenzie and Donald Mann, promoters of the Canadian Northern Railway, and in 1914 the route formally became part of the CNo system itself. By the 20s it been absorbed by the Canadian National Railways, which formed a separate company to run its system of electric railways. The Canadian National Electric Railway, as the subsidiary was called, modernized the NST, and added a new terminal on Geneva St in St Catharines.

Despite CN's ownership, the auto age inflicted the usual toll. In 1931, the Lakeshore line into Niagara-on-the-Lake was cut back to Port Weller, and in 1947 the Thorold to Niagara Falls route was abandoned. That year also saw the end of main line passenger service, and the change from electric power to diesel for freight. Passenger service on the Port Colborne branch continued into 1959, making it Canada's last radial passenger service. Eventually, the lines were cut back from Port Dalhousie to St Catharines in 1964-5, and from Port Colborne to Welland in 1962. The last portion of line to be lifted was that between Merriton and Welland.

Most stations built by the NST were single storey wooden buildings with shallow sloping rooflines. Such structures were located at

Fonthill, Welland, Humberstone, Niagara-on-the-Lake, and Thorold. The Port Colborne station was located in the original GT station at the corner of Elm and Kent east of the canal until 1925 when a new CN station was opened west of the waterway. The Merriton station was built of stone and brick and added a small turret on one corner.

The grandest building of all on the system was the Tower Inn Terminal at the Falls View Bridge in Niagara Falls. Built in 1928 in a chateau style with Tudor gables, it contained a restaurant and gift shop, and was topped off with a stone observation tower. While it stood, it was one of the Falls' most attractive structures and considered to be the most outstanding radial railway station in North America. However, in 1938, the Falls View bridge was destroyed by ice, and the location became a backwater. The stone terminal was demolished two years later.

 **All Aboard**

As with most interurbans, the rights of way tended to follow the shoulders of existing roads. With paving and widening, most evidence of these routes were obliterated. However, where they followed private rights of way, some evidence does remain.

This route goes from port to port, with a side trip into Niagara-on-the-Lake.

Take Lakeport Rd into Port Dalhousie. While no evidence remains of the railway on either side of the harbour, the port offers much history for you to see. Its revitalized main street faces the preserved lock from the second Welland Canal, while around the corner, now an ice cream parlour, stands North America's "smallest" jail. (The towns of Tweed and Creemore make similar claims.)

Nearby, Lakeside Park still offers refreshing respite form the peninsula's hot summers, only now people must drive, for the radial cars have long vanished.

Between the port and St Catharines, the rights of way have been paved over or built upon. However, an interesting little vestige can be found in John Page Park, on Scott St at the corner of Secord Dr. Here, now surrounded by grass, are the stone abutments of the bridge which

The main terminal for the NST in St Catharines was torn down to make way for a mall.

once carried the tracks over the old Welland Canal. While roadbed and canal have long vanished, the stonework appears almost like a sculpture in the open park.

From Port Weller to Niagara-on-the-Lake, the tracks followed the shoulder of Lakeshore Rd, and can occasionally be discerned as the CN tracks have only recently been removed from the side of the Port Weller bridge. In Niagara-on-the-Lake the tracks came in on Mary St and then along King. The extraordinary width of these two streets is testament to this heritage. And on King St, opposite the historic Prince of Wales Hotel, the old station still stands, with a bay window and little tower later added.

King St was most unusual in that it contained not one but two sets of tracks, for running down the opposite side of the roadway were the rails of Michigan Central, on their way to a wharf station. The MC right of way can also be seen at Charlotte and Promenade Sts, running along the east side of Concession One most of the way to Queenston.

To continue on the port to port route, return to St Catharines and follow Ontario St south to the bowling alley near Manchester Ave. Behind the building, along the bank of Twelve Mile Creek are the abutments of the bridge which carried tracks over the valley of the

A post card view shows the cars of the NST calling at the Thorold station. It too has gone.

creek. Then from Thomas St one block east of Ontario St, the tracks followed the shoulder of Louise St to Welland Ave, although no trace remains today.

From Welland Ave take Woodland St north to Railway St where the Terry Fox Trail now follows the right of way of the former Welland Railway. Sadly, the second of the NST's St Catharines stations, which stood at Geneva and Welland, was demolished to build a small mall.

Some sidings still occupy the old NST line in parts of St Catharines. However, the next place to see old vestiges is in Thorold which you reach by following Merritt Rd south from Queenston St. In the centre of Thorold, Merritt Rd becomes Ormond St, a block west of which is Front St and the historic downtown. The NST ran behind the stores on the west side of the street, but the right of way is now the site of a laneway, a bus terminal and a parking lot.

The station formerly stood where Beaver Dams Park now sits. While the park proliferates with plaques commemorating Laura Secord, Arthur Whelan, and the Battle of Beaver Dams, there is nothing about the community's railway heritage. It is a dereliction found in far too many towns and villages which owe their origins and their prosperity to the railways.

From Beaver Dams Park, follow Ormond St around to Beaverdams Rd and turn left. After a short distance, the abandoned roadbed of the NST crosses the road and runs along the left side. Beaverdams Rd then crosses Highway 406 to merge with Merrittville Rd which bends south to meet Highway 20. Turn right and follow Highway 20 to Station St in Fonthill.

Here the right of way, although grassed over, remains evident on the west side of the street. The little station which once occupied the site was moved off to become a storage shed near the town swimming pool, but has since been demolished.

From Station St follow Port Robinson Rd west to Pelham Rd (RR 36), and follow it south to Woodlawn Rd in Welland. Between Fonthill and Welland, the Stephen Bauer Trail now occupies the right of way. At Woodlawn Rd it is known as the Stop 19 Pathway where an informational plaque commemorates 20 years of Welland Transit Service. From here it continues as a trail to the north bank of the Welland River, where the bridge has been removed and the trail ends. South of the river, a small siding still occupies the NST roadbed.

Welland began as a busy railway junction. Here the tracks of the Welland Railway crossed those of the TH and B, the Michigan Central and the Grand Trunk. While the various reroutings of the Welland Canal have caused much track relocation, an old railway hotel yet stands on King St near the former site of the THB station. On Main St, and throughout the City, magnificent murals adorn the sides of stores, schools and shopping malls, some of which celebrate the town's railway roots. South of the main part of town, a neighbourhood known as Dain City marks the one-time junction of the Welland Railway and the Grand Trunk, where an attractive turreted station stood until the 1970s.

From Welland follow West Side Rd (Highway 58) south to Forks Rd, which you take east to Elm St and turn south. The route of the NST lay along the west side of the road, although most evidence has long gone. While the NST's two early stations at Humberstone and Port Colborne have vanished, a few more short blocks leads into Port Colborne where the large brick CN station still stands, now a restaurant. As mentioned in Chapter Ten, this lake-side harbour is a good place to enjoy the shoreline ambience, and connect with the route of the BBG either east to Fort Erie or west to Dunnville and beyond.

13.

The Niagara Falls Parks and River Railway, The "Great Gorge Route": Chippewa to Queenston

Far too many municipalities in Ontario who owe their prosperity to the railways, ignore that heritage. The few that celebrate it stand out. It is therefore ironic indeed that one of Ontario's shortest lived and least significant routes should enjoy the celebrity that it does. And that route is Niagara Falls' "Great Gorge Route". Thanks for that go, not to any municipalities, but to the Niagara Parks Commission for their thorough effort in plaquing the various features along it.

Like most things about Niagara Falls, there's an American side and a Canadian side to the railway. And the Great Gorge Route is no different. The Canadian side came first, of course, incorporated in 1891 by E.B. Osler of Toronto and R.B Angus of Montreal. It began operation in 1893, and within two years was carrying a half million passengers in a single year. Ferries from Buffalo landed at Slater Dock south of Chippewa, from where the trolleys rocked and rolled by the brink of the gorge, to Queenston where passengers could board a steamer to Toronto. The spectacular alignment gave passengers a dizzying view of the Horseshoe Falls, the American Falls and the turbulent gorge.

Naturally, the Americans were not about to be left out of such a lucrative venture, and in 1899 the Niagara Gorge Railway was built along the bottom of the gorge from Lewiston to Niagara Falls, U.S.A. At the same time a new bridge opened connecting Queenston with Lewiston. The temptation was too great. The two routes were quickly linked and a belt line known as the Great Gorge Route was soon attracting tourists from around the world.

In 1915 the worst accident on a Canadian radial line occurred at Queenston. As the car, badly over-crowded with Sunday picnickers, began down the steep incline from the Brock Monument, the engineer tried to release sand onto the tracks to help brake the wheels. To his shock, someone had forgotten to fill the sand box. With no traction for the steel wheels to grip, the car careened out of control and plunged into the river. Fifteen were killed and more than 100 injured. Had the steamer *Chippewa* which had been berthed nearby, not steamed out to the rescue, the death toll might have been far greater.

The auto age soon arrived. As it did in so many other places, it devastated anything that ran on rails. Between 1928 and 1932 ridership plunged, and the NPRR closed. The American side lasted a little longer. But the final blow there came in 1935 when a massive avalanche crashed down upon 65 m (200 ') of track. The cost of repair just wasn't worth it, and the era of viewing the Niagara River falls and gorge from the luxury of a streetcar seat were over.

 All Aboard --

While there are few visible remains on the NPRR, the parks commission has avoided the temptation to simply forget the route. Plaques at several locations serve to remind many of the long lost railway. In fact this route begins with a plaque.

About 2.4 km south of the community of Chippewa, just south of the falls itself, sits a plaque to commemorate the start of the NPRR at Slaters Dock. It is located on the river side of the Niagara Parkway Road. Nothing remains of the dock itself, however, except a wide and somewhat uneven grassy area between the road and the river.

From the plaque proceed north on the Niagara Parkway (which, by the way, also hugs the scenic shoreline of the river south to Fort Erie) to Bridgewater St in Chippewa. Then turn right at Portage St to cross the bridge over the Welland River. The hydro lines mark the site of the bridge that carried the NPRR cars over the river and to their next stop behind the MC railway station. This location is on the northwest corner of Front and Norton Sts. While the alignment of the now abandoned MC line, more recently lifted, is overgrown, the route of the NPRR is grassed over.

Return to the Niagara Parkway via Front and Macklem Sts. At the

Dufferin Islands, the road crosses the little waterways on a bridge which replaced the old railway bridge. A short distance further, in front of the power house, the western lanes of the parkway occupy the ground where the rails formerly lay.

The parkway then passes another power house, which lies to the west, on a bridge which once carried the NPRR. You then reach the entrance to the Table Rock "people mover" stops. These shelters stand where the NPRR power house once stood, while the Table Rock restaurant and gift shop, with its access to the tunnels behind the falls, were once a stop on the NPRR. The current Table Rock House was built in 1926, during the last years of the NPRR, replacing an earlier structure built in 1899.

The tracks were located on the west side of the older portion of the building, roughly where the public washrooms are now.

The right of way along the American side of the Niagara River is now a hiking trail, barely visible from the Whirlpool aerial car.

The tracks then paralleled the walkway beside the cliff to an attractive and delicate shelter at Inspiration Point. This little structure sadly has long vanished. However, the stone shelter at Ramblers Rest still stands, looking just as it did when trains, rather than cars, rumbled along the lawns beside it.

The next stop was for the ticket office for the Maid of the Mist and the incline railway to the water. This towered brick structure was considerably more appealing that the somewhat functional concrete box which replaced it. Another plaque marks the site of Rainbow Bridge which carried the Belt Line cars back and forth over the border, until a devastating ice floe swept it from its footings sending it crashing into the river below. Here too stood the beautiful Tower Inn Terminal for the Niagara St Catharines and Toronto Railway (see Chapter 12).

Beyond this point the tracks followed the east shoulder of the road up to the Bridge St station located below the Michigan Central railway bridge which still carries both passenger and freight trains high above the gorge. The NPRR station, however, is long gone.

A short distance after the bridge you come to the Whirlpool. This marks the site of not just a small station shelter and ticket office for the aerial car, but also the location of the NPRR car barns. Today, a new

Top: A NPRR car passes the station and ticket office for the Maid of the Mist.

Above left: The route which the NPRR followed into Queenston has changed little over the years.

Above right: The Niagara Glen gift shop occupies the only surviving *in situ* station of the Great Gorge Route.

ticket office, gift shop and large parking lot have obliterated all traces of the streetcar heritage.

From the whirlpool car and lookout, you can see, on the American side, a pathway beside the river. This represents the American portion of the Great Gorge route, and is now a hiking trail.

Continue along the Niagara Parkway to Whirlpool Rd. Note that the route is nearly ½ km back from the river. This is due to the presence of a mysterious hidden gorge which once carried the waters of the Niagara River, until it was filled with debris from the great melting ice sheets some 20,000 years ago. This blockage forced the mighty river to seek another outlet, the 90 degree turn which you see at the Whirlpool today. The only vestige of the hidden gorge was a gully known as Bowman's Creek, across which the NPRR constructed a trestle. While that trestle has long since been filled in, another plaque commemorates the structure. Nearby, a few of the old abutments still protrude above the grass.

The next few meters of road are located away from the brink, while the NPRR remained closer to the lip itself. A short distance further along, the Niagara Glen gift shop is located in the only NPRR station still in situ. This solid storey and a half stone structure has changed only slightly in the years which have followed.

Near this spot you will also find another former NPRR station. Relocated to the driveway which leads to the Horticultural School, it is the former station and gift shop from the Brock's Monument stop.

From Brock's Monument, the tracks of the NPRR paralleled the parkway down the steep escarpment, cutting to the west and then swinging back east to enter Queenston, parallel to Clarence St. Here you will come upon a dead end road which marks the route of the old Highway 8 and the abutments of the vanished Queenston-Lewiston bridge.

From Kent St in Queenston, one set of tracks led to the bridge, while two others led north to the site of the dock. One set followed a dirt lane opposite Dumfries St, another passed via Deep Hollow north of Walnut St, also now a dirt lane. The dock is still there, but now it is used by fishermen, and no longer by radial passengers awaiting their steamer.

14.

Line to the Lake, the Lake Simcoe Junction Railway: Stouffville to Sutton

One of the main goals of Ontario's early railway builders was to tap the hinterlands. Here lay the timber, the minerals and the barley, all vital to Ontario's fledgling economy. The first railway lines were usually anchored at a lake port from which point they would wend their way to wherever their charter, and their funding took them. Often, that wasn't far. A number of lines were simply portage lines which connected existing lake ports.

While the Toronto and Nipissing Railway (which never even remotely approached Lake Nipissing) wound from Toronto to Coboconk, it still lacked a portage connection. Accordingly, a feeder line was proposed from a point on the TN to Lake Simcoe, then a key transportation route for Ontario's early settlers and lumber companies. This would give them the portage route they sought.

The Lake Simcoe Junction Railway began at Stouffville, a booming town set amidst some of Ontario's best farmland, and terminated at Sutton, with a spur line extending to the wharf at Jackson's Point. Water tanks were located at Mount Albert and Sutton, while engine houses were situated at Sutton and Stouffville. Eight stations and sidings were located along the line. Stations built at Sutton and Mt Albert were to be identical to the two storey wooden station at Stouffville (demolished in the 1970s), that at Blake (Brown Hill) was to be patterned after Kirkfield (still standing), while the remaining stations would repeat the style of the single-storey wooden TN stations at Woodville, Eldon and Markham (the latter now restored with the help of the federal Millennium fund).

Train service on the LSJ was not particularly frequent. The two daily mixed trains were reduced to one after just three years of operation,

The Jackson's Point extension of the LSJ was short-lived, thanks to the arrival of the Toronto and York Radial Railway. The station became a shelter at the lakeside park.

however, a full passenger train was running by 1910. By 1917 it was back to just one mixed train a day. Then, due largely to competition from the Lake Simcoe excursion trains run by the Toronto and York Radial Railway, service was cut back from Jackson's Point to Sutton. In the meantime, another railway line, that of the Canadian Northern, was built from Toronto northeasterly to pass Lake Simcoe on the east side, and parallel to a portion of the LSJ route. In fact, both lines were nearly adjacent to each other in Mount Albert.

By 1928 the newly formed Canadian National Railways had assumed both lines and undertook a major relocation. By eliminating a section of the LSJ line between Stouffville and Zephyr, it could move the junction from Stouffville closer to Sutton to a point on the former Canadian Northern line near Zephyr itself. Then, in 1928, the CN eliminated passenger service to Sutton, although occasional freight service was maintained until the entire line was abandoned in 1979.

 All Aboard --

The route starts at the intersection of Edward and Main Sts. in downtown Stouffville. Although CN demolished the Stouffville station in the 1970s, the community's railway heritage has been rejuvenated.

From the new commuter station on Stouffville's main street, the hard working volunteers of the York and Durham Heritage Railway have restored summer train service to the historic Uxbridge station on the original TN route. While Stouffville heartily supported the venture, the politicians in Uxbridge, caving to a tiny anti-train lobby, forced the operation to reduce its 1999 schedule, a short-sighted move which reduced revenue to both the train and to Uxbridge businesses.

While appreciation of the railway heritage on the TN line is strong, that along the LSJ has all but vanished. Although the newer branch from the former CNo line to Sutton is now a snowmobile trail, the original alignment, between Stouffville and Zephyr, is only occasionally visible.

In Stouffville, the only reminders of the railway's earliest days are the former hotel, now a restaurant, and the grain elevator a short distance along the track. The junction itself is no longer visible. To see the right of way, drive north to Bloomington Road, where, just east of the intersection with Highway 48, the right of way appears as a lane and a fence crossing on a southeast-northwest angle.

The first station north of Stouffville was that at Ballantrae. It stood west of Highway 48 on the north side of Aurora Road, and was a flag stop with a freight shed and living quarters for the section foreman. It was a smaller version of the Markham station.

North of Ballantrae came the station at Vivian. While the right of way south of Vivian Road and west of Highway 48 is no longer visible, it can still be traced leading north from Vivian Road. It was here that the station, a clone of that in Ballantrae, stood. It burned in 1919, and was replaced with a small waiting room.

From Highway 48 follow Herald Road west to Franklin Road. Now largely vanished, Franklin began as a grist mill town which grew to include two general stores, two blacksmiths, two sawmills, and houses for its 150 residents. But because the town of Mount Albert was so close, the LSJ never constructed a station in Franklin, designating the location instead as a flag stop named Powells.

Today, all industries have vanished, and only four original homes line the side road. The LSJ embankment however is clearly visible as it angles across the Franklin Road a short distance north of Herald Rd.

Located at Highway 48 and Mount Albert Road, the thriving town

Top: A railway shelter still stands in the tiny lakeside park at Jackson's Point.

Above left:: One of the few communities along the LSJ to celebrate its railway roots is Brown Hill, where the former railway hotel is plaqued, and the park named after the station.

Above right: Sutton's last station was moved to Georgina Village Museum where, along with other local historical buildings, it has been preserved.

of Mount Albert could once claim two railway stations. The first, that of the LSJ, stood west of King Street near Albert, approximately where the Home Hardware now stands. The more recent Canadian Northern station stood at the end of Princess Street until it ceased operation and was moved to a park in Cannington.

Centre Street leads north out of Mount Albert to Queensville Sideroad where, a short distance west, the right of way has been incorporated into a hunt club driveway.

The new junction sits at Zephyr Road and Uxbridge Concession Road 1. While the route of the CNo has become CN's main line to the west, the newer LSJ right of way has become a snowmobile trail.

The one community on the line to retain a modicum of its railway heritage is the community of Brown Hill. Originally called Blake Station, the village still contains the railway hotel, complete with an historical plaque. The open green area opposite the hotel represents the site of the station, a two storey building like that still standing in Kirkfield, the siding and the stockyards. The area is called, fittingly, Brown Hill Station Park. The small grid network of village streets retain a few houses of railway vintage, although new homes now dominate the area.

The only station to survive the days of rail along the LSJ was that in Sutton. The original LSJ station was replaced in the early 1900s by one with a Grand Trunk style similar to that still standing at Kinmount. When it burned in the 1920s, it was in turn replaced with a standard CN plan station. After the line closed it was moved to the Georgina Village Museum a short distance west of the town on Base Line Road.

Because it grew to become a busy resort town, and more recently a dormitory community for Toronto, Sutton's railway relics are hard to find. The station grounds and the site of the turntable and engine house were, at the time of writing, an overgrown lot west of Dalton Road and north of Base Line Road. New development is being proposed for the site.

The short-lived extension to Jackson's Point is harder still to locate. The route followed Park Road, and then Lorne Street where a linear park represents the right of way. Following the closure of the extension, the small Jackson's Point station was moved to the lakeside park where it served for a few years as a shelter. Two other railway shelters still stand in the small park.

15.

The Grand Trunk's Washed out Railway; Oshawa to Port Hope

It had been the Grand Trunk's original plan to locate its line far inland from the lake in order to most effectively compete with the established lake shippers. For this reason, stations at places like Kingston, Belleville, Cobourg and Oshawa were placed three to four km (2 - 3 miles) from the water's edge. In other cases, where the topography further inland was too steep, a shore route was the only choice. From Port Hope to Port Union, the route, for the most part, ran right along the water's edge. Access to the water also enabled construction workers, equipment and supplies to arrive by boat at places like Port Hope and Port Britain in order to build the line.

But by building so close to the lake's waves, tracks and road bed alike sometimes washed away. One of the first sections to be moved inland was a five-km or three-mile stretch of track between Port Hope and Cobourg. This was completed in 1859, just three years after the line was opened. Known as Duck Harbour it extended between what the railway designated as mileage 265 and 268.

But a far more extensive relocation was that of the exposed section of line between Port Hope and Oshawa. For about five km (three miles) west of Port Hope the tracks followed the beach itself before swinging inland. Here, during the Grand Trunk's extensive double-tracking program at the close of the century, a total of 10 km (six miles) of track between Port Hope and the Newtonville station was relocated further north. While some of the work was done to avoid erosion, other portions were moved to avoid expensive cutting and filling which the double tracking would have entailed.

Further west, between Bowmanville and Oshawa, an eight km section (five and a half miles) was relocated southward. Already far enough inland to avoid lake erosion, this move was simply to allow the construction of a new double track through more level terrain. To double track the existing route would have meant more cutting and filling, a much more costly alternative.

Three stations were affected by the move. The station at Port Britain was closed entirely, while those from Newtonville station (also known as Wesleyville Station) and Darlington were moved to the new track. As a result, Newtonville Station and Port Britain have became virtual ghost towns. While both settlements are occupied today, they are relic villages, their glory days behind them.

Although the portions moved represented only a small portion of the Grand Trunk's Montreal Toronto line, so much was moved between Port Hope and Oshawa, that it has all the appearances of a ghost railway. At the very least, it does reveal a long-lost episode in Ontario's railway lore.

 All Aboard --

Although the current line through Oshawa still follows the Grand Trunk's original route, the community of Cedardale has lost its railway identity. At the time of construction, what is today's Oshawa consisted of three little settlements, Port Oshawa on the lake, a mill village a short distance inland, and on Kingston Road, the other main transportation route, the settlement of Skae's Corners. When the Grand Trunk route was placed about halfway between the road and the lake, a station village named Cedardale was laid out around the little stone station. The small network of roads included Nonquon Road, now Simcoe St, leading to Port Oshawa, Margaret St and of course Station Street, now Albert St.

Oshawa's growth during the 20th century overwhelmed the railway village. When the current station was built at a new site on the western end of the city in the 1960s, the old station was removed. Little evidence of its existence can be found today. Nevertheless, several early buildings, including former stores and residences, still stand on Cedardale's streets.

To access the abandoned portion of the early right of way east of

Built too close to the waters of Lake Ontario, the Grand Trunk's original embankment has a gap where waves have washed it out.

Oshawa, follow Base Line Road east from Courtice Road (exit 425 on the 401) to Rundle Road. A line of hydro poles which cross Rundle Road south of Base Line Road indicate the location of the old road bed. For about a kilometer or so, the road bed is clearly visible from the 401 itself and runs adjacent to the fence line on the north side of the highway.

Continue east on Base Line Road to Green Road. A short distance south, the road bed stands out as an embankment on the west side of the road, and as a prominent cutting on the east. The current track was relocated to the south to avoid the expensive cutting and filling which double tracking the original alignment would have entailed at this location.

For many years one of the more beguiling landmarks for 401 travellers was an oddly isolated stone arch on the north side of the highway just west of Bowmanville. This was an original Grand Trunk bridge which carried those first tracks over a farm lane. Overlooked and neglected, this historic landmark was removed in recent years.

The current line through Bowmanville remains true to the original routing. While the old station was demolished in the 1960s, the railway hotel, a handsome red brick building, still stands beside the station

The new CN tracks pass within metres of the original Grand Trunk alignment, and the station village which was known as Newtonville (or Wesleyville) Station.

grounds at the foot of Liberty St.

To reach the next portion of abandoned road bed, follow Bennett Road south from the 401 a short distance east of Bowmanville. An early cut is evident in the hill east of the road, while on the west there still remains a small stone abutment from the overpass that carried the line across the road. West of that however, most of the embankment has been removed, leaving only small isolated knolls in the fields.

Again, in the vicinity of Newcastle station, the two rights of way mesh, although the site of the Newcastle station, a simple wooden structure, is vacant and overgrown. East of Newcastle, the two road beds once again split. From Newcastle drive south to Bond Head where you will find several early buildings, including one-time hotels, that date from the community's heyday as a busy lake port. At its peak in the 1880s Bond Head was shipping 70,000 board feet of lumber and 24,000 bushels of wheat. Today only a few of the 50 or 60 houses still stand, while a public beach occupies the ground once covered by the mills and warehouses.

From Bond Head follow Lakeshore Road east. One of central Ontario's most scenic short drives, it follows the lake and mounts craggy headlands, giving extensive views along the shore. After crossing

This former street-car once stood beside the Grand Trunk right of way at the flag stop of Willow Beach a short distance west of Port Britain.

both the CP and CN tracks on a single wooden bridge, another example of a disappearing railway legacy, the road swings east to parallel the tracks. South of the tracks a line of old telephone poles represents the location of the original right of way.

After crossing the tracks again, this time at a level crossing, look on the west side of the road for a gate. This gate marks the old roadbed where a small railway culvert can be seen. Continue on Lakeshore Road, passing through the ghost town of Port Granby, another former lake port where warehouses and grain elevators have been replaced by private dwellings.

Continue to Townline Road and follow it north. A pair of old houses on the east side of the road a short distance from the turn marks the site of Newtonville (also known as Wesleyville) station. The more northerly of the two dwellings was the station master's home, while the stone foundations of the station lie, almost indiscernible, in the grove of trees behind it. The former road bed is now a private lane just a few meters from the current CN line.

Return to Lakeshore Road and continue east. This brings you into the ghost village of Wesleyville with its vacant school and early church. Further east, just beyond the flashing light at the entrance to the for-

This stone bridge once carried the Grand Trunk's original tracks over a farm lane. Urban sprawl has eliminated both the farm lane and the bridge.

mer Wesleyville generating station, the road glides down a gentle grade. Off to the south are the waters of the lake and along the shore, clearly visible, the embankment of the old route. Gaps in the embankment mark the locations of the washouts which prompted its relocation inland at this point.

Willow Beach Road leads to the lake and an old white house which contains a railway name board announcing "Willow Beach". The property is private here, but the old right of way is clearly visible on both sides of the road.

The next road is the Port Britain Road and the location of a once busy milling centre and shipping point. The Grand Trunk placed its small wooden station by the lake, while hotels, stores, and private homes clustered around the intersection of Lakeshore Road and Port Britain Road. During the mid-1800s, when it was an important lake port, Port Britain contained two hotels, a grist mill, saw mill and carding mill, as well as a tannery, two stores and a wagon maker. The townsite consisted of 100 lots and a population of 350.

Although the tracks are long gone, and the cove where the schooners called is now quiet, several historic buildings, including a former hotel, and several early houses, mark this forgotten port. The

GT road bed remains visible at the end of Port Britain Road, altered now to accommodate private driveways, but there is no evidence to reveal where the station once stood.

East of Port Britain, the embankment can be seen clearly from the road and continues close to the lake. Lakeshore Road then passes beneath the current tracks of both the CN and CP and enters Port Hope.

A fitting finish to this route, Port Hope remains one of Ontario's best-preserved historic towns. Mansions, workers' homes, town hall, theatre and main street all retain a remarkable heritage integrity. And down by the lake, the old stone Grand Trunk station continues to serve train passengers as it has since 1856, making it, some claim, Canada's oldest, continuously operating railway station. Much of the exterior stone work was restored during the 1980s, while the small waiting room has been refurbished in a turn-of-the-century fashion. The station is now used primarily by commuters to Toronto. Carrying the tracks high over the harbour is the Grand Trunk's original stone bridge.

If you linger in Port Hope, you will also find two other ghost railways, both featured in *Ghost Railways of Ontario: Volume One*. From the foot of John Street, a pedestrian walkway traces the roadbed of the former Midland Railway. Where the path reaches Walton St, Port Hope's main street, the doorways at the rear portion of Len's Travel mark the Midland Railway's Walton Street station.

Further north, on Ontario Street, you can see the intricate red brick building which served as the Canadian Northern's railway station. Unfortunately, Port Hope lost its red brick CP station during that railway's "demolition derby" of the late 1970s.

16.

The Thousand Islands Railway; Gananoque to Gananoque Junction

Some may argue that, at two kilometres, or one and third miles, Muskoka's "Portage Railway," the Huntsville and Lake of Bays Railway (see Chapter 22) warrants the title as Ontario's "shortest" ghost railway. The TIR after all was twice as long. Although it did have its own charter, the HLB was in reality nothing more than a shuttle service between two steamer wharfs. It served no stations, and had no customers along the line. The TIR had both.

From the beginning, Gananoque was an important location along the St Lawrence. Its water power attracted mill owners as early as 1787. By 1808 it was a stage stop on the Montreal to Kingston road, and had a steamer wharf by 1819. But by the 1840s, when American railways began to make incursions into Great Lakes shipping, Gananoque business became concerned over becoming a transportation backwater. To respond to that economic threat, they lobbied for a railway for the Canadian side of the river.

The first route, proposed by the Montreal and Kingston Railway, would pass as much as 16 km or 10 miles inland from the river. It was an alignment which, predictably, invoked howls of protest from Brockville and Gananoque, ports which would have been bypassed. In response, the government gave the charter instead to the English-financed Grand Trunk Railway. Their proposed route, closer to Kingston and Brockville, appeased those communities, however topography would still keep the route five km (three miles) inland from Gananoque.

The GTR did however build a Gananoque station, and it was one of their fine stone arch stations of the type that still serves Prescott and Port Hope. But the road to it remained almost impassible, and the community continued to agitate for a rail link.

A TIR train at the new Gananoque Junction station.

The first glimmer of hope came in the 1870s with a proposal to build a line, to be called the Gananoque and Rideau, from the town wharf to Merrickville, some 40 km (30 miles) to the northeast with a branch line to Westport, and a possible ferry link to the American railways at Clayton, New York. The line would be built and operated by the Grand Trunk, with local funding. However, as so often happened, the funding fell short, and the arrangement was terminated.

By the 1880s however, the giant lumber firm of A.S. Rathbun, operator of the Bay of Quinte Railway (please see *Ghost Railways of Ontario: Volume One*) had acquired property along the Gananoque waterfront and, under the charter of the Thousands Island Railway, built the vital link to the Grand Trunk station themselves. The first train ran the route on December 15, 1883.

At the junction of the two railways, a small settlement named Cheeseborough grew. Here were the Rathbun buildings, station, section house, living quarters for the section foreman and station agent,

The TIR bridge in downtown Ganonoque has been planked for pedestrian use.

and John Thompson's hotel. A combined station office and engine house was built at the wharf, while a passenger platform was constructed at King St, Gananoque's main thoroughfare.

In 1899, responding to the boom in tourism, the Grand Trunk proposed a larger, more elaborate station about two and a half km, or a mile and a quarter east of the existing junction. The new station would measure 16 m by 7 m (50' by 20') and would be topped with an octagonal tower above the agent's bay window, while mullioned glass would be fitted in the transoms above the doors. A large awning would provide shelter during the peak summer season. The Grand Trunk trains would use the north side of the station, the TIR the south side. Meanwhile, an attractive little umbrella station was constructed to shelter passengers waiting at King St.

One part of the TIR-GTR agreement was that the TIR had to meet every GT train that stopped at the Junction, a provision that later helped hasten the demise of the line. Nine trains a day operated along the line, and during these heady days, carried more than 45,000 passengers a year.

In 1929 a new station was built at the wharf, an attractive brick building with pillars and a bell caste roof, with a small Tudor gable above the

The TIR's wharf station was converted into a gift shop and restaurant before burning down in 1990.

entrance. By this time, however, the highway age had arrived and the road system was being improved. Bus service was inaugurated along what would later become Highway 2, and passenger travel on the TIR plunged to fewer than 7,000 by 1931. Although the line lost money nearly every year after that, the TIR was still required to meet every train arriving at the junction. By the 1950s it was averaging just one passenger per trip.

A decade later passenger service ended, and freight service was reduced to one train a day. In 1970 the wharf station was converted to restaurant, and in 1978 the CN threatened to demolish the station at the Junction. Brushing aside pleas to save the station, a CN official declared "If the building has historic significance I'm not aware of it." Indeed, during the 1970s and 80s, a dismal era of rampant station demolition, both of Canada's major railways seemed totally oblivious to the heritage significance of this country's railway stations. Happily, when VIA assumed Canada's rail passenger service, it renovated the building, and trains continue to stop there.

They are, however, no long met by the trains of the TIR. In 1995, the last industry on the line ended its rail requirements, and the line was abandoned.

 **All Aboard** - - - - - - - - - - - - - - - - - -

The little umbrella station and TIR engine remain a landmark in downtown Gananoque.

Despite its short length, the route of the much legendary TIR offers much to see. The town of Gananoque has remained proud of its railway heritage and has retained many features of the old railway. Most evident is the little green and white umbrella station which stands beside the museum on King St. The museum itself is housed in an early hotel, one that catered to railway travellers. Beside the umbrella station rests TIR engine number 500. A gas electric engine, it hauled the cars of the TIR from 1931 until 1966. Across the road the former TIR bridge over the Gananoque River has been decked in and serves now as a pedestrian walkway, as does the River Street bridge.

Along the right of way historic structures such as the Stones mill, which predated the TIR, still stand. The waterfront itself, however, has been radically altered. Following a fire in 1990 which destroyed the wharf station, new shops and parks replaced the tracks and sidings. Here tourists wait to catch the popular Thousands Islands tour boats, shop or enjoy a meal. The only significant building to survive from the railway age is the former customs house.

Between Gananoque and Cheeseborough, the right of way sits abandoned, awaiting re-use. County Road 35, Station Road, leads three kilometers (1.85 miles) from Highway 32 to the Junction station. Here, on the south side of the newly clapboarded station, some TIR track remains in place, as well as portions of the TIR platform. Further west along Highway 32, Pineview Road leads to the site of the first junction station where only a single building remains from the village of Cheeseborough.

Gananoque remains one of Ontario's most historic and heritage-conscious communities, and the TIR will always remain part of its story.

17.

Ontario's Drowned Railway; Cardinal to Cornwall

Some of the most historic sections of Canada's most historic railway now lie below sea level, or more accurately, below Seaway level. In 1958 the St Lawrence Seaway's new system of dams and locks between Cardinal and Cornwall was complete, and the waters began to rise. As they crept higher, those waters began to engulf the locks of the older seaway. The inundation poured into the foundations of the historic Loyalist towns that once harbored refugees fleeing the American Revolution, and then lapped the right of way of Canada's first major railway project, the Grand Trunk. Although the Seaway was an engineering marvel, and a much needed transportation system, it obliterated from the landscape nearly two hundred years of history.

One hundred and two years earlier an equally ambitious scheme was completed, the building of the Grand Trunk Railway. In 1856 trains began running between Montreal and Toronto. In order to more effectively compete with the lake shippers, the builders of the GTR located their stations well back from the shore, often as far as two to three kilometers (one to two miles). The cost of bridges and fill which would have been needed for a route closer to the shoreline was also a factor in the inland alignment.

Stations were located at intervals of roughly nine to 12 km (six to eight miles) depending upon the demands of both farmers, and steam locomotives. Many were handsome stone structures with shallow pitched roofs and rows of arched windows. Along the St. Lawrence stretch such stations were constructed at Prescott, Lancaster, Cornwall, Morrisburg, Lansdowne and Gananoque Junction. A similar but larger structure was built of brick at Brockville, a divisional point.

While most trains were through trains, a local train between

The Aultsville station has been preserved near the popular heritage park, Upper Canada Village.

Brockville and Montreal was inaugurated Oct 16, 1856. Because it was a favorite with the Mohawks of the St. Regis reserve near Montreal, it was nicknamed the "Moccasin."

Through the 1950s, as the plans for the new Seaway neared completion, it became evident that the colourful little riverside communities were doomed, and the railway would need to be relocated. The new route took it even further from the river, passing primarily through swamps and young forests. Stations, which had for a century served the communities of Iroquois, Morrisburg, Aultsville, Farran's Point, Wales (the station for Dickenson's Landing), Moulinette and Mille Roches, would be replaced with more modern buildings at the "new" communities of Morrisburg, Iroquois, Ingleside and Long Sault.

While the old Grand Trunk stations at Moulinette and Farran's Point were simple wooden shelters, those at Aultsville and Mille Roches were larger wooden operator stations. The Wales station was a solid brick building, while that at Morrisburg was one of the GTR's classic stone stations. The GT station in Cornwall was an expanded version of the standard stone stations. While several of these building sites were inundated, others were not. The original location of the Morrisburg station remained well inland from the new flood line, yet the building was removed anyway. Similarly, the old stone station at Cornwall, although in no danger of being "drowned" was also replaced with a newer building a few blocks further north.

The five new stations were uniform in style, a modernistic flat-roofed pattern with extensive use of glass and decorative brick. Double entry doors lead into spacious waiting rooms with open ticket counters, parcel lockers and telephone booths. The four local stations at Long Sault, Ingleside, Morrisburg and Iroquois measured about 24m by 7m (60' by 20'), while that at Cornwall was more than 50 m by 14m (150' by 40'). It remains the only one of the five where VIA Rail passenger trains still call. The Morrisburg station stands, but is in private use, while that at Iroquois is vacant and heavily vandalized. Those at Long Sault and Ingleside have gone.

Fortunately, most of the new shoreline has remained open to the public as part of the St. Lawrence Parks system, and the vestiges of the "drowned railway" are evident in many locations.

 All Aboard -

The route begins in Cardinal where Station Road leads east from CR 22 to the station grounds. In keeping with the GT's standard practice, the station was situated a couple of miles from the river and the community it was intended to serve. As a result, a small settlement grew near the station. While only rubble marks the site of the wooden station today, a couple of early rail era buildings, likely boarding houses, still stand. East of the road's end, the current rail line now bends slightly to the northeast marking the point at which the new alignment and the old diverged.

Between Cardinal and the "new" town of Iroquois, the right of way has been turned over to private property owners and converted to private lanes. In Iroquois, the Carmen House museum, located in an 1815 stone house, marks the location of the former right of way. The original village of Iroquois stretched for about a mile along the river east of the house, with the station being located at the easterly end of the village. The station grounds are now part of a golf course. At the east end of Iroquois, the right of way is now Dr Miller Drive which

The Grand Trunk's handsome brick station at Wales served the community of Dickenson's Landing.

extends as far east as an early cemetery. Beyond this point the alignment becomes a trail through a marsh.

East of Iroquois, CR 2 bends south to follow the right of way itself. A few yards before it joins the historic route, a railway bridge abutment becomes visible in the marsh a few meters south of the road. All the way to Morrisburg, the highway has buried the old route, nowhere yielding any clue as to its former use. The "Welcome" sign in Morrisburg represents the former location of Morrisburg's fine stone station.

The appearance of "new" Morrisburg is disappointing, a faceless suburban commercial development which could be anywhere. Happily, a large portion of old Morrisburg remained above the water mark, but nowhere are there any vestiges of the historic Grand Trunk.

That all changes a few kilometers east of Morrisburg. Here CR 2 once again swings northeasterly and away from the former right of way. A short distance past the new community of Riverside Heights, with its numerous relocated buildings, Crysler Beach Road leads to

The flag station from Moulinette has found a new home in the Lost Villages Museum grounds.

one of only two stations to survive the inundation, that from Aultsville. The right of way itself passes a short distance in back of the station, while in front, a Grand Trunk engine and some vintage passenger cars commemorate the passing of the historic "Moccasin" train.

To reach the site of the original station grounds continue east to the Aultsville Road and follow it south until it bends east. Continue straight south from this point along a stretch of old asphalt to where a distinct hump marks the former crossing. A badly overgrown sidewalk is as close as you'll get to the station site itself, however. The road then crosses a swamp beyond which stood the site of the doomed village, considered by many to have been one of the prettiest of the Loyalist towns.

East of the Aultsville Road, the highway again runs close to the river, while offshore, the right of way remains visible in the shallow water. Farran's Point Road marks the location of the Farran's Point station. In Farran's Point Park, two km (a mile and a quarter) east, a walkway follows the right of way for a couple of kilometers.

A few kilometres east, the highway passes Union Cemetery, south of which stood the Wales station, a brick building built in the same style as that from Aultsville, and located to serve the village of Dickenson's

A one-time causeway on the drowned railway has kept above water near Ingleside.

Landing. Only divers now can explore the underwater sites of Dickenson's Landing, Moulinette and Mille Roches.

Landlubbers, however, can still see the former Moulinette station. A small flag station, it has been preserved and relocated to Lost Villages Museum park, along with several other historical structures from the area.

Seven km (4 ½ miles) east of the park, CR 2 enters the sprawling and unattractive City of Cornwall. Here squats the massive Seaway dam, which is responsible for the flooded land behind it. Below it, and back on dry land, the old right of way contains two small sections of rail. Now a spur line, one such section provides access to the pulp mill and other nearby industries from the new CN line a short distance away. Cornwall Junction, as it was called, also marked the junction of the GT with the New York and Ottawa, later New York Central line, now abandoned, which led from New York state to Ottawa (please see *Ghost Railways of Ontario: Volume One*). Rosemount Ave leads to this location. In the east end of the city, east of 10th Street, and McConnell, a CN storage siding leads west from the new main line and occupies the track of the drowned line.

Through the rest of the city, however, the right of way lies buried under pavement and shopping malls, particularly where it ran beside 9th Street. Sadly, the lovely old stone station was demolished to be replaced by one of those malls. The only building to survive from the days of rail at this location is a former hotel, now a Hooters tavern.

Efforts by local heritage groups to save Cornwall's historic buildings have generally met with little enthusiasm from local politicians. Besides losing all three of its old stations, Cornwall's city council also authorized the demolition of the community's early atmospheric theatre, one of the few then still surviving in Ontario.

Among Cornwall's few surviving historic sites, are Inverarden, an early Regency cottage house now occupied by the United Counties Museum. Near the river, at the west end of the city, you can still see the remains of locks from the Seaway's predecessor canal.

18.

The Peanut Line, CPR's Cornwall Connection: Cornwall to St. Polycarpe

Over the years of the golden age of railways, Ontario witnessed the chartering, the incorporation, and the construction of hundreds of small railway lines. In the early years most actually operated as independent lines until economies forced them to amalgamate. But there were dozens of other railway companies, independent on paper, that were in fact subsidiaries of the large companies. The Peanut line was one of them.

By 1910 the CPR had been limited in the number of railway charters which could be granted to it. But they remained anxious to add to their network of branch lines. One method to get around this was for private individuals to simply establish a company on paper, obtain a charter and hopefully funding, and then lease the line to the CPR for 999 years.

This was the unsavoury beginning of the CPR's Cornwall connection.

From the start, the Grand Trunk had obtained a virtual monopoly along the north shore of Lake Ontario and the St Lawrence River. When it decided to follow the lake shore, the CPR was forced to build further inland, missing such key ports as Kingston, Gananoque and Cornwall. To obtain the lake access which it needed, the CPR, in the case of Kingston, took over the Kingston and Pembroke Railway, an established resource railway.

In the case of Cornwall, it was forced to create a dummy company. That company was known as the Glengarry and Stormont Railway. Its charter terms spelled out a 40 km (29 mile) route from St Plycarpe Jc in Quebec on the CPR's Montreal main line, to Cornwall where it would establish junction points with the GT and the New York

Like all Cornwall's other historic railway stations, that of the CPR was demolished.

Central's Ottawa branch. The latter is likewise a ghost railway, and is featured in *Ghost Railways of Ontario: Volume One.*

The line was completed in 1915 and was leased almost immediately to the CPR. Stations were located at 7 points. Besides Cornwall and St Polycarpe, there were stations at Bridge End, North Lancaster, Glen Gordon, Williamstown, and Glenbrook. Passenger service included a daily mixed train from Montreal to Cornwall.

While the "Peanut Line", as it was called locally, connected with both the GT and NYC, it never made it as far as the harbour in Cornwall. Rather, it terminated at a modest station at the corner of Pitt and 6th Streets where it also erected a turntable, engine house and freight shed. Passenger service ended in 1952, and the line itself was lifted in the late 1990s.

 All Aboard --

While the right of way remains clearly evident, having not, as of this writing, been disposed of, the Peanut Line has otherwise left few vestiges.

The only known surviving station from the Peanut Line is that from Glenbrook, now located in Williamstown.

This route begins in Cornwall near the corner of 6th and Sydney. While Cornwall has considerable railway history, it has no railway heritage. All three of its historic railway stations, that of the CP, the New York Central, and the original stone station built by the Grand Trunk, have all been removed. Aside from material gathered by the well run United Counties Museum, local politicians and most citizens have turned their backs on their railway past. That is why the former CPR station grounds, hidden behind a Food Basics store, are simply a vacant and overgrown field now, with no vestiges of any railway structures at all.

The tracks of the Peanut Line crossed those of the GT beside Tenth St just a short distance west of McConnell St . Here a rusting CN siding is all that remains of the GT's drowned line (see Chapter 17). The new CN bypass can be seen a short distance north.

To leave Cornwall and follow the Peanut Line, follow Tenth St east to Boundary Road and turn north. Continue on until you reach CR 19 and turn east.

After about 7 km the road passes through the hamlet of Glenbrook. The station stood about one km south of the main intersection in the hamlet, and is the only one from the Peanut Line known to survive. To locate it continue on CR 19 into the historic town of Williamstown. Follow Herron Rd north from the centre of town, just before you reach the bridge. The station, a small Swiss Cottage style, lies about 3 km north and is now a private dwelling, with only minor alterations to its exterior appearance. Along the way you will pass the old railway bridge, still in place.

To reach the Williamstown station grounds cross the river and follow CR 17 to Track St. The old two storey wooden western style station has long gone leaving only a vacant lot. Despite this, Williamstown is one of those delightful little eastern Ontario villages which time and tourists have happily passed by, leaving it little altered by modern day development which has blighted so many of Ontario's townscapes.

You will also find in Williamstown the Sir John Johnson house, now a National Historic Site. Johnson was a British military hero in the American Revolutionary war, and assisted many United Empire Loyalists to flee persecution in the U.S. You can also visit the Nor'westers and Loyalist Museum, or the historic Bethune Thomson House.

The next little country station stood at Glen Gordon. To reach it go back into the centre of Williamstown and take CR 19 north to Cedargrove Road and turn east. The right of way appears beside the road as you arrive at the stop sign for CR 34, and the site of the country station. No evidence remains here of station or railway buildings.

From the south side of the right of way, drive east from Highway 34, to a T-intersection where you turn left and drive about four km (2 ½ miles) to CR 26 where you turn left again. After less than 2 km you come to the right of way at North Lancaster Station and what was a small boarding house or hotel. A laneway opposite the building leads a short distance to the site of the station grounds.

Continue north on CR 26 to the hamlet of North Lancaster and turn right onto CR 18. At CR 23 turn south for a km to a mound that marks the Bridge End station grounds. While the junction lies east along Route 340 near De Beaujeu in Quebec, if you continue north on CR 23 into the village of Dalhousie Station, located just inside the Quebec border, you will see a rare railway water tank, one of the few to still survive. With its unusual stone base, and red wooden tank, it is also one of the most photogenic.

Although on the still-active CP main line, this picturesque water tank in Dalhousie Station is a rare survivor.

Aside from the vestiges of the Peanut Line, a few unusual historic attractions can be found in the area. South on CR 34, the historic community of South Lancaster is an early port on the St Lawrence and contains many early 19th century buildings on its network of narrow streets. North on Highway 34 is Alexandria with its operating VIA station, a handsome brick building with hip gable roof, and across the road the old station hotel. A short distance west of CR 34 on CR 18, the old Montreal Road, lies one of Ontario's few European-style ruins, the stone shell of the Cathedral of St Raphaels. Gutted by fire in the 1970s, the 19th-century walls have been stabilized, and, although roofless, the Cathedral still holds religious pageants.

19.

The CPR's South Shore Line, St Eugene to Ottawa

As early as 1853, Montreal railway promoters were anxious for a direct link to Ottawa. In that year a charter was given to the Vaudreuil Railway to build to Ottawa from a link with the Grand Trunk on the St Lawrence River west of Montreal. No action followed, however, until 1887 when it was renamed the Vaudreuil and Prescott Railway. In the meantime two Ottawa links had been constructed, the Quebec Montreal Ottawa and Occidental, which followed the north shore of the Ottawa River, and the Canada Atlantic Railway which crossed the Grand Trunk at Coteau on its way to Ottawa, soon to be the nation's capital.

Furthermore, the CP added yet another line of its own, that connecting Montreal with Smith Falls. Nonetheless, the CP, which by then had acquired the VR's charter, went ahead with the south shore railway. Now called the Montreal and Ottawa Railway, it was opened between Vaudreuil and Rigaud in 1890. But instead of linking with the Grand Trunk at Vaudreuil, as originally planned, it connected with CP's Smith's Falls line at the same location.

Another change to the original plan was to move the route inland from the Ottawa River, rather than follow the shore of the river. The latter alignment was subsequently taken by the upstart Canadian Northern Railway (please see *Ghost Railways of Ontario: Volume One*).

In 1897 M and O was opened as far as Alfred, and two years later puffed into Ottawa itself. After first using the Broad Street station built by the QMOO, the trains began calling at the CAR's Central Station opposite the parliament buildings. This was subsequently replaced by the Grand Trunk's new Union Station, which stands to this day. Built in 1912, it was converted to a conference centre in the mid-1960s when

Most CP trains entering Ottawa used the Broad St Station before switching to the new Union Station in 1912.

Ottawa's current railway station was opened, and is now off limits to the public.

Between Rigaud and Ottawa trains called at 13 stations: St Eugene, Stardale, Vankleek Hill, McAlpines, Caledonia Springs, Alfred, Plantagenet, Pendleton, Bourget, Hammond, Leonard, Navan, and Blackburn.

Primarily a passenger route, the M and O bought two new passenger train sets boasting satinwood panels and columns, and plush seating. Most of the freight between Ottawa and Montreal went by way of the older north shore route. Few of the towns along the M and O had much in the way of industry, most being farm towns.

Then, with the opening of Highway 417 between Ottawa and the Quebec border, and with VIA Rail operating passenger trains on the nearby CN tracks, the M and O South Shore line became redundant. By 1986 the line was abandoned and soon after the rails lifted as far as the fine stone station in Rigaud, Quebec, from which Quebeckers can enjoy commuter rail service into and out of Montreal.

 **All Aboard** ---

The right of way, at this writing, remains abandoned along most of its route, its disposal still to be determined. Most of the stations were built according to CPR's western plan station, with a combined freight and passenger facility, and a small dormer above the agent's office for his bedrooms. Following the CPR's "scorched station" policy of the late 1970s and 80s, most of these solid stations were ripped down. During this administration it became the CPR's practice to demolish all redundant stations. Where facilities for CP employees were required, the railway replaced the fine old buildings with aluminum trailers. Pleas from countless municipalities and heritage groups went unheeded, as the CPR carried out the most prolific station removal initiative in the history of the province. Only two of the M & O's Ontario stations survive, that at Bourget, still on site, while the single storey Stardale station became a storage shed behind a house.

By contrast, the surviving stations in Quebec, at Hudson and Rigaud, were individually designed and survive as commuter stations.

Between Rigaud and St Eugene, the M and O's first Ontario station, the right of way runs straight and level across the fertile farmlands of the lower Ottawa River valley. St Eugene is a small French farm village which straddles County Road 10. With siding and station both gone, there is little evidence of the community's railway days.

The section from St. Eugene to Stardale presents much the same image, a straight right of way past flat fields. To reach the site of the Stardale station, turn north from County Road 10 just after passing over Highway 417. No buildings remain at the lonely one- time crossing. However, the station was moved to a farm a short distance north to serve as a storage facility. It was a single storey wooden station whose bay window area has now been covered over.

The line continues westerly, crossing the still active short line of the L'Orignal Railway. Vankleek Hill station contained yards and a small settlement, as well as the standard western plan station. The building survived until the late 1980s when, despite the pleas of local citizens, the CPR demolished it. Today only an overgrown yard marks the spot, as do the buildings of the settlement

The Plantagenet station, like most on the CPR's South Shore line, was a "western plan" structure. Like nearly all the others, it has gone

Vankleek Hill itself is a well-preserved town of solid red brick houses and stores, many of the latter still with their white wooden balconies, a trade mark of Franco-Ontarian architecture. To reach Vankleek Hill retrace your steps south from Stardale to County Road 10 and follow it west to Highway 34, the main intersection in downtown Vankleek Hill. The station grounds are two kilometers, or about a mile and a quarter, north of the town on Highway 34.

To reach the next station stop, McAlpines, continue west from Vankleek Hill on CR 10 to CR 20 and turn right. A couple of railway buildings mark the former crossing. Stay on CR 20 to reach Caledonia Springs about 8 ½ km (five miles) further along. This one-time spa now consists of rural sprawl where modern homes stretch along the road, while a pair of early structures mark the crossing and station grounds. Here the right of way is blocked off to prevent vehicular access.

CR 20 leads to CR 15 which in turn leads west to Highway 17 and Alfred. Continue through the sprawling village to CR 18 and follow it south three km (two miles) to the site of Alfred Station. It is worth noting that CPR located their stations at some distance from the communities they were intended to serve. Higher land costs in the village

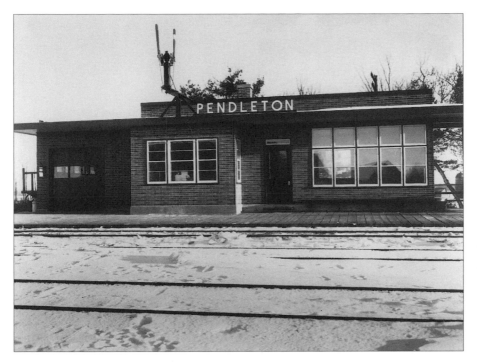

The station at Pendleton was built using a post war "international" style, popular with railways during that period.

areas, which the CPR was reluctant to pay, usually accounted for this inconvenience. The Alfred station was a lonely sight surrounded by farm fields. No settlement developed here.

Plantagenet Station, by contrast, did consist of a small settlement, with a few village streets, sidewalks and some handsome historic buildings including a red brick former hotel. A short distance east of the station site the CPR crossed the South Nation River on a solid iron bridge which is still in place. To reach the site turn left from Highway 17 onto CR 9 and follow it into the village of Plantagenet. At the junction with CR 26 follow CR 9 to the left. The station village lies about 2 ½ km (1 ½ miles) south of this intersection.

Pendleton, the next station site, lies about eight km (five miles) further west. Continue south from Plantagenet Station to CR 2, then west to CR 19 and south again to the next crossroads, just beyond which lay the station. The last station here was a more modern flat-roofed building built in the post-war international style. Nothing remains at the site today.

The little cross roads settlement of Pendleton itself lies less than two

The only station to survive *in situ* is that at Bourget.

km south. The most direct route to the next stop is west from the station grounds to Highway 17 and west another six km (four miles) to Bourget. Turn north in the centre of this busy rural village to Rue Levis and follow it west along the right of way for less than a kilometer (a half mile) to, shockingly, a real station. The Bourget station somehow evaded the CPR's station wreckers and stands today on site, little altered. Even its name board remains in place. Like most along the line it is a western plan station with a dormer above the bay for the agent's apartment.

Continue west from Bourget to CR 21 and then north to Hammond where urban sprawl has overtaken the site of the station. As throughout this route, the right of way remains in an abandoned state. Continue along CR 21 north for four km (about three miles) to CR 1, which becomes RR 28, then west eight km, or five miles, to CR 35 and finally south for two km, or a mile and a half, to Leonard.

Now almost a ghost town, Leonard contains on the west side of the road a pair of early rail-era buildings, while the overgrown station grounds themselves lie on the east side of the road.

Return to RR 28 and follow it west to Navan. Continue west through the village's main intersection on Smith Road which leads to the station

Following its closure, the wonderful stone station at Carleton Place stood boarded up until it reopened as a day care.

grounds about 1 ½ km west. The stop signs on the right of way indicate it is a snowmobile trail in this area. No early railway structures or rail-era buildings, however, have survived. After passing Blackburn, the right of way once more boasts tracks which lead into Ottawa's station. These however have been assumed by CN and link with its still active Montreal line.

West of the present-day Ottawa station, CP track carried on in a westerly direction eventually joining its oldest route, that of the Canada Central at Carleton Place. The route through Ottawa however was replaced with the Queensway in the 1960s, while the line from the west end of Ottawa to Carleton Place was removed only in the early 1990s. Despite some interest in converting this latter section to a commuter rail line, the rails have been lifted, and much of the route is now a road.

Two stations have managed to survive from this section. The small wooden portable station from Ashton now rests in a private yard in the village of the same name a short distance south of the right of way, while the fine stone station at Carleton Place is now a day care centre, and remains on site. The Ottawa Valley once contained several similar stone stations — at Pembroke, Renfrew, Arnprior, Almonte, and Perth, however despite the efforts of these communities to save these historic buildings, the CPR demolished all.

20.

The Ontario and Quebec Railway, from Peterborough to Perth

The most striking feature of the land through which the abandoned right of way of the O and Q passes, is its stark ruggedness. Low ridges of rock, some of the oldest and hardest in the world, defied railway builders and discouraged settlers. Villages were few and far apart, and in many stretches, farms were non-existent.

Nonetheless, the promoters of the railway were determined to build a trunk line through this hostile land. The financial benefits of a long route which gathered traffic from its branches had brought in millions to the Grand Trunk, which ran well to the south, and the Great Western railways, both of which had been operating for nearly three decades.

By connecting the Canadian Pacific's Perth-Montreal branch in the east, with the Credit Valley Railway in Toronto in the west (with its connection to Michigan via the Canada Southern in St Thomas) the O and Q could bridge an important gap between the American mid-west and the ocean port of Montreal. It would create a monolith to challenge the mighty Grand Trunk, hitherto Ontario's only province-wide trunk line.

From its junction with the CVR at West Toronto, the line crossed Yonge St, near today's Summerhill Ave, a point which was then north of Toronto. Here the O and Q built a handsome brick station which it named Yorkville, after the closest village of any size. It then sliced through the farm of one William Lea, where the station was named Leaside, a name later passed along to a town site laid out, ironically, by the rival Canadian Northern Railway.

The route then took it northeasterly through Agincourt, then easterly, well north of Lake Ontario, where the route of its rival Grand Trunk lay. After winding through fertile farmlands, it entered

The O and Q station at Bathurst was built in what was called the "Van Horne" style, and was copied at almost every station along the line.

Peterborough where it added another station in the style of its Yorkville depot. East of Peterborough, the land became increasingly harsh until at Havelock the O and Q established a divisional point with yards and a roundhouse.

The line stubbornly continued east, snaking around unrelenting rock ridges, and bridging frequent swamps and rivers, finally breaking through into the flat farmlands of the Ottawa Valley and the CP branch line in Perth. Along the way, the O and Q crossed no fewer than eight north-south railway lines.

Aside from Peterborough and Yorkville, the O and Q used identical stations. Simple two-storey wooden structures, they were nick-named the "Van Hornes" for the style that the irrascible CPR railway builder, William Cornelius Van Horne, placed almost everywhere across the prairies.

A Toronto bound dayliner prepares to leave the Havelock station mere months before the Brian Mulroney government eliminated the popular service.

Then in 1908, the CPR built a rival to its own line. This was the lakeshore line built through the same Lake Ontario communities which the Grand Trunk once called its own. The new route met the tracks of the O and Q at Glen Tay, a short distance west of Perth. Traffic on the O and Q declined, and by the 1950s, of the stations between Havelock and Perth, only those at Maberley, Sharbot Lake, Kaladar, Tweed and Bonarlaw survived. Finally, in 1971, the rails between Tweed and Glen Tay were lifted, and in 1988 cut back to near Havelock itself.

 ## All Aboard --

The route starts in Havelock, 29 km east of Peterborough on Highway 7, which parallels the right of way at various distances for its entire length. Currently the end of rail for the O and Q (although track extends a few kilometers east to serve a 3M plant at Preneveau), Havelock remains a delightful railway town where historic cafés and hotels still line the road opposite the yards. Although much less busy than they were, the yards are still filled with mining cars hauled from the nepheline syenite mines at Blue Mountain and Nephton to the north. The handsome brick station, with its steep roof, and which replaced the original wooden station in the 1930s, still stands and is now in private hands. Visible from well down the highway, it stands as the village's main landmark.

One surviving eatery is the historic family-run Station House Restaurant. More a café than restaurant, it is clean, friendly and chock–full of railway memorabilia. You can park in the large parking lot beside the yards where the community has been busy adding flower beds and otherwise generally beautifying the place.

The next station was called Blairton. Located 7 km to the northeast of the OQ station, the original village of Blairton is now a ghost town. Having boomed on the backs of a large deposit of iron ore, it was the terminus of a very different railway line, the Cobourg Peterborough and Marmora, later renamed the Cobourg, Blairton and Marmora Railway . One of Ontario's first railways, the Cobourg and Peterborugh Railway crossed Rice Lake on a trestle. When the crossing proved unstable, the railway re-routed from Rice Lake to the large iron deposits at Blairton, and replaced the trestles with a barge. But by the end of the 19th century, the deposits had become uneconomical, and the population at Blairon plunged from 500 to fewer than 25. The CPM was abandoned.

The O and Q station grounds are located on Methuen 14th Line, about a few metres south of Highway 7. Here the trackless right of way is an open trail, beside it a former section house. Much less visible is the long abandoned CPM right of way, barely evident another half kilometer (quarter mile) south.

Highway 7 continues east into the historic community of Marmora. Here you can explore the ruins of Ontario's first iron foundry, built in the 1820s. A much later mining operation, that of Bethlehem Steel which operated between 1951 and the early 1970's, left a gaping open pit, now filling with water. It yawns beside an overgrown look-out point east of Marmora.

In Marmora, Highway 7 crosses the Crowe River, where Memorial Park displays the original Marmora station. Built by the Central Ontario Railway (for more information, please see *Ghost Railways of Ontario: Volume One*), it was closed and relocated in the late 1980s.

Today the site of the Bonarlaw station is marked only by two intersecting snowmobile trails.

To reach the next OQ station site, turn south onto CR 14 at the main intersection in Marmora and travel 8 km, or five miles, to the small community of Bonarlaw. Here the COR and the O and Q crossed with the single- storey wooden depot wedged between the two tracks. Station Road leads west from the highway a short distance to the overgrown station grounds. Although no evidence remains of the station, or any other railway structures, the two rights of way are now open trails.

To reach the next O and Q station site, continue south on CR14 to Springbrook and follow CR 38 east to Highway 62 and the roadside hamlet of Ivanhoe. The right of way lies at the south end of the settlement marked by the one-time railway hotel, a two-storey white building on the east side of the road.

Return north from Ivanhoe to resume County Road 38 east. At Crookston, a short distance along, the Madoc branch of the COR crossed the O and Q. A scenic road, CR 38 winds through rugged pasture land, here and there displaying the log buildings of early pioneers. Between Ivanhoe and Tweed stood a small siding known as Buller, but nothing remains to mark the spot.

An attractive lakeside village, Tweed marks the crossing of yet anoth-

Now a ghost town, Sulphide was a busy mining town on the O and Q.

er north-south line, that of the Bay of Quinte line (please see *Ghost Railways of Ontario: Volume One*). While the BQ station has long gone, and the right of way paved over, the O and Q station still survives as of this writing. Now a lumber office, it has been little altered, and retains its exterior wood siding and tuscan red paint. The only O and Q station to survive on site between Havelock and Perth, it is located on Colborne St, east of the main street.

The main street, incidentally, is where Tweed's boosters claim to have North America's smallest jail. Now a tourist office, it measures just 4.8 m by 6 m. Tweed is not alone in this regard. Other pretenders to having the smallest jail include Creemore and Port Dalhousie. A short distance south of Tweed, the community of Stoco retains its BQ station, likewise still on site.

From Tweed the Sulphide Road leads east to the ghost town of Sulphide and the site of another small station, built to serve this once–bustling mining town. A single- storey "Swiss Cottage" style station, it served as a private home until the 1980s when it disappeared from the landscape. Less than three km (two miles) east of Sulphide, a residential lane leads north from the dirt road to the section village of Hungerford. Only a handful of small homes mark the location.

Return now to Highway 7 by backtracking through Tweed and following Highway 37 north to the community of Actinolite.

A Phantom Railway

Here, near the junction of the two highways, a small picnic ground on the north side of the road contains the stone abutments of the phantom Toronto and Ottawa Railway. Originally proposed in 1874 as the Huron and Quebec Railway, the line would link Toronto with Ottawa via Peterborough, Sharbot Lake and Perth. By 1881 it had been renamed the Toronto and Ottawa line, and 13 km, or 8 ½ miles, between Madoc and Actinolite were graded, with a bridge built across the Skootamatta River. A further 100 km (62 miles) were partially graded between Actinolite and Perth, a route followed today by Highway 7. Near Silver Lake and Weymiss, the highway uses the original embankments and road cuts built by the TO. By 1883, however, the Midland Railway had gobbled up many smaller lines, including the charter of the TO, and the line was scrapped before any trains had travelled it.

From Actinolite to Kaladar, Highway 7 winds through some the most difficult terrain in central Ontario. Low rocky ridges and interminable ponds and swamps line both road and rail line. An historic marker just east of Highway 41 tells of the hardship of settlers taking what was the Addington Road north to their farm lots. But it tells nothing of the railway. As with all too many communities on this and on other Ontario ghost railways, rail heritage is ignored.

Kaladar began as a stopping place of the Addington Road, and the community's few early buildings cluster around this intersection. The station site lay along Station Road, which leads east from Highway 41 a short distance south of 7. Although nothing remains of the station — even the site is difficult to recognize — the right of way itself remains an open trail, as it does through most for its length.

Highway 7 continues through harsh terrain for another 10 km (six miles) to Elm Tree Road, where, just east of the right of way crossing there stood yet another long-lost station. An early pioneer trail, Elm Tree Road winds its way east, passing log cabins and early pioneer hotels as it does, before crossing the Salmon River near the railway hamlet of Ardendale. Where land was unavailable or too expensive in existing settlements, railways would build their stations some distance away, and around them small satellite communities would grow. With nowhere to build in the mill town of Arden, the O and Q located their station a few miles west and named it Ardendale. The dirt lane to the grounds leads to the right a short distance after the road crosses the river. Today Ardendale consists only of a pair of early dwellings, and the rail trail.

Once a bustling mill town, Arden itself is now a backwater, and almost a ghost town. Along its small grid network of streets, some of them overgrown, old hotels and stores sit boarded up, while the mill itself has become a dwelling. Despite the aura of near-abandonment, most homes remain occupied.

From Arden drive south to the first road east, marked "Mountain Grove." This scenic lane winds around lakes, and past pioneer farms before swooping down into the busy community of Mountain Grove. Although only a hamlet, Mountain Grove contains a pair of churches and a new school. While buildings which date from railway days include the store and a couple of hotels, now dwellings, no evidence remains of the station or of any other railway buildings. The right of way parallels the road a short distance south.

From Mountain Grove, the paved road leads north back out to Highway 7. Fourteen kilometers (8 ½ miles) further east lies the resort town, and once- busy railway junction, of Sharbot Lake. Here, for a short distance, the O and Q and the Kingston and Pembroke Railway (please see *Ghost Railways of Ontario: Volume One*) shared tracks and a station.

Follow Highway 38 south from 7. Elizabeth Street leads west from Highway 38 to the lake, and the site of the station which is now largely forgotten, marked only by a small pile of broken asphalt. At the south end of the town, a bridge and causeway, bearing the date 1928, carried both lines across a narrows in the lake.

Between Sharbot Lake and the next station at Maberley, there stood another now indiscernible siding named Ungava. From Maberley on Highway 7 follow Bobs Lake Road south a short distance to Maberley Station Road which ends at the right of way. The lane to the station, Station Siding Road, is now a private driveway, but a short stroll along the rail trail from the public road soon leads to the old station grounds. While the station has long gone, the former hotel/boarding house stands on a rise of ground a short distance back. Littering the right of way are the rusting wheels of an old jigger. A few other rail-age houses are located along the road as well.

Another 12 kilometers (7 ½ miles) along Highway 7 leads to the site of Bathurst Station, where the original "Van Horne" depot was replaced with a smaller "Swiss cottage" style structure. Nothing remains at the station grounds, however the newer station is now a dwelling, little altered, on the north side of Highway 7 a short distance east of its original site. At Glen Tay the shining rails of the newer Lakeshore line appear on the south side of the Highway, and mark the CPR's current Montreal main line.

While the handsome stone station at Perth was reduced to rubble during the CPR's notorious anti-heritage regime of the 1970s and 80s, that at Smiths Falls, a divisional station on the CP's historic Canada Central line, appears to have been rescued. An agreement reached between CP, VIA Rail and the town, will recycle the building. Unlike the appalling lack of interest along most of the O and Q, this example is a fine testimony to a railway community which has also converted its former Canadian Northern station into a railway museum.

21.

The Bracebridge and Trading Lake Railway : A Phantom Railway; Bracebridge to Baysville

By the close of the 19th century, Ontario was enmeshed in a spider's web of railway lines, with more to come. But more numerous than the lines which criss-crossed the province, were failed attempts which did not. For every line built, there were three which never made it off the pages of the charter. The Bracebridge and Trading Lake Railway was one.

In 1875 the tracks of the Toronto Simcoe and Muskoka Junction Railway (later the Northern Extension Railway, and then the Grand Trunk) reached the shores of Lake Muskoka, and eliminated at last the jolting journey by stage coach over the primitive Muskoka Road. Suddenly, tourists could travel in comfort and transfer from the trains at Muskoka Wharf station onto the steamers which would glide over pine scented lakes to the grand new lodges.

Railways also meant more industry and more money. Little wonder that investors wanted as many steel rails as they could coax governments to finance. Speculators hurriedly laid out towns in eager anticipation of tracks coming their way. Some, like Huntsville, shared that boom. Others, like Hoodstown on nearby Lake Vernon, boomed briefly, then died when the railway surveyors passed them by.

In 1886, when the railhead arrived in Huntsville, investors wondered how to link the line with Lake of Bays (the new name for Trading Lake). The nearest tracks were at Bracebridge on the Northern Railway (two years later it would become part of the Grand Trunk) 30 km, or about 20 miles, to the west, and at Kinmount on the Victoria Railway more than 60 km (almost 40 miles) to the southeast.

Two rival schemes were proposed. One would see a link by steamer from Huntsville across Peninsula Lake, and then by a short portage railway to Lake of Bays with a terminus on its north shore. The other would be by an all-rail branch from Bracebridge to Baysville.

At first, the BTL seemed to have the upper hand. Baysville was a larger community—there was no community on the north shore—and the all-rail scheme would eliminate the problem of winter freeze-up which would hamper the portage line. Furthermore, the topography which confronted the portage route was more difficult than that which would be followed by the BTL.

In 1892 the ground-breaking for the BTL seemed imminent. Led by local steamship operator, A.P. Cockburn, the BTL group secured a federal subsidy of $2,000 per mile, payable, however, only after construction started. Not to be outdone, Huntsville steamship owner, George Marsh, quickly included the portage line into the charter for his new steamship company. An economic downturn in the 1890s delayed both projects, but by 1903 the portage line had secured enough funding to proceed, and in 1904 went into service.

But the promoters of the BTL were not dissuaded and continued their search for funds. They were banking on the lumber industry as customers, a source not available to the smaller narrow gauge portage line. Finally, in 1906, with the on-again-off-again government funding at last in place, construction of the BTL actually began, even though private funding remained elusive.

From Bracebridge the route would follow the twisting valleys in the hard bedrock along the north bank of Sharpe Creek to Fraserburg, and then follow the valley of the South Muskoka River into Baysville. Despite the hopeful beginning, funding continued to pose a problem. While government money remained available, private sources never materialized. Following a few miles of grading in the Baysville area, construction sputtered to a halt.

New promoters, H.P. Dwight of Northwestern Telegraph, and William Brown, a Baysville sawmiller, tried to resuscitate the line, but with no more success. By 1912 the line was dead.

Had it been built, the landscape of Baysville would have been far different than it appears today. Wharves and industries would have lined its lakeshore, while hotels and restaurants would have appeared near the station. Fraserburg would have received a small station as well.

But by the 1950s, the lumber era was over, and the auto age had arrived. Private cottages replaced the grand hotels. In 1959 the Portage Railway closed, as, no doubt, would the BTL, had it been built. And it too would have joined the ranks of Ontario's ghost railways.

The old Bracebridge station would have been the western terminus for the BTL phantom railway.

 **All Aboard** ---------------------

Today the route proposed for the BTL remains a scenic backwater. Muskoka Road 14 follows what would have been the rail line from Roxborough to Fraserburg. Here you can stop and photograph the delightful log church at Roxborough, or proceed further east to search out the lost settlement of Monsell (please see *Ghost Towns of Ontario: Volume Two*)

No road, however, follows the proposed alignment which would have linked Fraserburg with Baysville. RR 14 leads instead into the lovely lakelands of Oakley township, and no further. Highway 117, further north, now provides the main artery between Bracebridge and Baysville, the railway terminus which wasn't.

Pause in High Falls park at the intersection of Highways 11 and 117 to see central Ontario's grandest waterfall, and the bridge abutments of the old Highway 11. On Lake of Bays itself, the elegant old Bigwin Inn evokes the nearly lost era of Muskoka's grand hotels, and that of the trains and steamers which once served them.

22.

A True Short Line: the Huntsville and Lake of Bays Railway; North Portage to South Portage.

Short lines, now the rage in the railway world, don't come much shorter than this...only a little over two km, or a mile and a third in length. Yet the Huntsville and Lake of Bays, or the "Portage Line," was economically one of the most important of Muskoka's early railways.

It all began when a Muskoka sawmiller named George Marsh entered the steamboat business and acquired a charter to provide steamer service to Peninsula Lake and Lake of Bays. With the arrival of the railways through Gravenhurst and Huntsville two decades earlier, Muskoka was quickly developing into a booming resort area. Grand hotels began to appear around the pine clad lakes. And the only way to reach them in those tranquil pre-auto days was by train and by steamboat.

While the Muskoka Lakes lay right on the main line of the Northern and Pacific Junction, later the Grand Trunk Railway, Lake of Bays, one of the region's most attractive water bodies, remained beyond the reach of the rails.

One proposal to remedy this was a proposal to construct the Bracebridge and Trading Lake Railway, an off-again, on-again route from Bracebridge to Baysville (see Chapter 21). While this line was sputtering, Marsh was working on ways to build a railway over the height of land which separates Lake of Bays from Peninsula Lake. Although only 1 ½ km wide, the land bridge presented a difference in elevation of more than 50 m (165'). As the terrain precluded a canal, a portage railway to connect the two steamer wharfs seemed the most practical solution.

In 1895 Marsh was granted his charter to begin shipping. In 1900 he

An early view of the Portage Railway.

received a second charter which specifically permitted him to start building his portage line which he named Huntsville and Lake of Bays Railway. Marsh's first idea was to construct an electric railway built to the standard railway gauge of 4' 8 ½" (or about one and a half meters). But because no source of electricity was readily available, the line was steam powered, while a narrow gauge of 3 ½' (a little over a metre) was chosen when it appeared that this was the only width of engine available.

In 1904 the little line was finished, and Marsh rode the first train. Just months later he was dead.

In its early years, the HLB railway provided the only means of moving people and supplies to the lakeside resorts But in later years, when cars, buses and trucks were more prevalent, the trip itself became more of an excursion than a necessary journey. Tourists would travel to Huntsville on the CN's Muskoka Express, stopping first at the wharf in Gravenhurst, and then at the station wharf in Huntsville. Here the steamer Algonquin waited to carry them to Fairy Lake and then through the canal to Peninsula Lake and the railway terminus at North Portage. Passengers would climb into one of two wooden passenger cars for the short lurching journey to South Portage on Lake of Bays.

Because the grade coming out of North Portage was quite steep, a heavily loaded train might not make it to the summit on the first try, and would return to the switchback to try again. If it didn't make it a second time passengers might be invited to walk. At South Portage, the *S. S. Iroquois* (later replaced by the *Iroquois II*) would carry them to Dorset while the Mohawk Belle operated between the portage and Dwight.

In 1947 the original saddle tank steam engines, nearing the end of their own line, were sold to an American collector, and replaced with two newer locomotives. But these years marked the beginning of the Auto Age. The roads to Muskoka were paved and tourists began to drive. This also marked the beginning of the end for the grand resort age, and the entire Muskoka shoreline became enveloped in a ring of private cottages. In 1952 the steamer *Algonquin* was retired, and the *Iroquois II* moved to Peninsula Lake. But it was taken out of service in 1959 and lived out its remaining days in Kingston. The Portage Railway lived on for another year regaling tourists with its novelty. But this could not pay the bills and in 1960 the famous Portage Railway fell silent.

The equipment was moved to Pinafore Park in St Thomas before returning to its home turf near Dwight. Now it runs again, once more regaling the tourists with its novelty, this time adjacent to the Muskoka Pioneer Village at Huntsville.

 All Aboard -

The little line hasn't really left much to see. The Northlander, now the only train to Huntsville, stops only at the main line station (until such time as the Ontario government ends the service), while pleasure boats instead of steamers follow the rivers and canals through Mary, Fairy, and Peninsula Lakes. The only vestige of steamer days in Muskoka is the historic Seguin, the last of the Muskoka steamers, which operates now out of Gravenhurst.

To reach the route of the Portage line, follow Highway 60 east from Huntsville to the Hidden Valley Road and drive to Portage Road. Turn south at Portage Road, which is RR 23. Near this intersection lies the

Top: The Portage line's last equipment has found a new home beside the Muskoka Pioneer Museum at Huntsville.

Above left: The old hotel at North Portage put up many passengers on the Portage Railway.

Above right: The scene at South Portage during the dying days of the Portage Railway.

vast and upscale Deerhurst Resort which traces its roots to the early days of the HLB steamers and railway.

Follow RR 23 6 ½ km to Wolfe Bay Road and then turn left to the water. The right of way crossses RR 23 just before this intersection. Drive to the water where you can still see the wharf and the building which housed the former North Portage post office.

At the intersection the Portage Inn still stands, restored in recent years, having provided accommodation for nearly a century.

Between North and South Portage, the right of way parallels RR 23 to the west, obscured by bush, until it crosses to the east side within sight of Lake of Bays, and the sister terminus of South Portage.

Many of its early buildings still linger, along with others of newer vintage. The site of the railway wharf lies beneath the cement of a larger and newer government dock, while through the bush the tiny right of way is mostly overgrown.

But the legacy of the Portage Railway lives on in print, in legend, and at the pioneer museum, if not on the landscape itself.

While in Muskoka, spend time in the pioneer village. Here you will explore pioneer buildings hauled in from the far corners of the region, including the former hotel from the ghost town of Spence, and the general store from the ghost town of Falkenburg. Railway relics too can be found throughout the region. While railway stations from Southwood, Martins Siding and Burk's Falls have been relocated to private lands, the historic station at Gravenhurst has been restored *in situ*, and fills a variety of functions. Sadly, the sturdy yellow brick Huntsville station has been left to deteriorate by both the CN and the Ontario government. A short distance north of Huntsville, the ghost town of Scotia marks the junction of the Northern and Pacific Junction Railway with the old Booth Line, the latter now a rail trail used primarily by snowmobilers. (Please see *Ghost Railways of Ontario: Volume One*).

23.

Rails Through the Park; The Canadian Northern from Pembroke to Capreol

The Canadian Pacific Railway was not Canada's only national dream, although it was the first. At the same time as the CPR was sending its trains across the new country called Canada, two determined entrepreneurs were setting out to accomplish on their own what had taken a national government, and a major conglomerate to accomplish—a railroad from coast to coast.

But their strategy differed from that of the CPR. Instead of grabbing government money to construct the route in one fell swoop, William McKenzie and Donald Mann cobbled together their empire by buying unused charters and underused lines. Starting modestly with a tiny branch line in southern Manitoba, they completed their Canada-wide iron link in less than twenty years. East of Ottawa the Canadian Northern passed along the north shore of the St Lawrence in Quebec, and across New Brunswick to Yarmouth in southern Nova Scotia. West of Capreol it continued on, deep into northern Ontario, before swinging back south to hug the shore of Lake Superior into Port Arthur. West of Thunder Bay it entered the Canadian prairies by way of Rainy River and Minnesota, reaching its terminus at Vancouver.

One of the key pieces of that route traversed the rugged and thinly settled Canadian Shield between Ottawa and Capreol. The most ambitious portion of the CNo, this section was built around 1914, and might well have been called the "sawmill line," for most of the towns and villages along it depended upon the presence of a sawmill for their existence. Others, especially those within Algonquin Park, prospered from tourism, while the unlikely little sawmill town of Brent, in northeastern Algonquin Park, became a railway divisional point, and developed into a community of some size.

But good farmland was found only in a few small pockets, and mineral resources remained scarce. Most of the other names along the line represented only sidings, water tanks or section hamlets.

By the 1920s Algonquin Park was becoming renowned for its rugged scenery, clean air and tranquility. The day of the logging truck was still, happily, in the future. To help generate revenue, the Canadian National Railways, which had assumed the CNo, began to promote tourism within the Park, even building its own lodges.

The Grand Trunk had started it off after it acquired John Booth's Ottawa Arnprior and Parry Sound railway through the southern portion of the park. When the CN took over both the GT and the CNo, it launched a promotional blitz of its own. "In the hearts of most men and women lies an instinct as old as humanity itself," crowed a 1920s brochure. "No other of Canada's famed playgrounds can more adequately answer to that desire than Algonquin Park."

The pamphlet goes on to tout the canoeing and the camping, the fishing and the resorts that lay along the old CNo. The Wigwam on Kioshkoqui Lake offered a log cabin lodge "with only the rough edges taken off," and "accommodation in tented sleeping quarters on raised wood floors." Near Agnone Station, Lake Traverse Camp, located "on a wooded knoll overlooks a sand beach and affords a charming view of the lake. The large central lodge comprises a dining room and lounge, while sleeping accommodation is provided in two-room cabins and tents on raised floors, each tent with roomy verandah surrounded by large fly." The area's wildlife was also a major drawing card. "The surrounding forest harbours moose, deer and bear, and the camera hunter (sic) finds many opportunities for securing wonderful still and movie pictures."

The Park also became a lure for some of Canada's most renowned painters. While working as a fire ranger, painter Tom Thomson lived in a small cabin at the Achray station where he painted his famed "Jack Pine".

Two rail-side communities near the north end of the park developed into sizeable towns, their destinies intertwined. Their names were Fossmill and Kiosk.

Fossmill is the older of the two. Begun as a small sawmill village by William Foster, Foster's Mills, later elided to Fosmill or Fossmill, was purchased in 1924 by the larger Fassett Lumber Company of Quebec which needed better access to market.

But the town would last only ten years. In 1934 a fire raged through the mill, utterly destroying it in less than 45 minutes. Fassett's owner, Sydney J. Staniforth, moved operations east 14 miles to Kiosk, the site of the J.R. Booth company's old limits and camp. Here there remained only a bunkhouse, office store and warehouse. While Booth's loggers had removed the white pine, they left the hardwoods, and that's what Staniforth wanted.

For several years, Fossmill's men commuted along the line to the new mill. But in 1946, when Fassett sold the old townsite for a mere $400, most moved to Kiosk. By the early 1950s the new village could claim a store, new church, school, and 75 houses.

Then in 1973, the mill burned. Because the Ministry of Natural Resources' new park plan prohibited mills and towns, Staniforth was forced to rebuild outside the park while the residents were given until 1996 to move. Although the residents did not go without a fight, the site today is a wasteland of rubble, overgrown lanes and weedy lots. Even Booth's historic boarding house was demolished in the name of "wilderness".

From the western boundary of the park, the railway veered north into North Bay where it became the third railway to enter town. The first to arrive was the CPR, acquiring a vast swath of land on the lake for yards and divisional facilities. Soon afterward, North Bay welcomed the Temiscaming and Northern Ontario Railway with its offices and repair shops. (The TNO never had a station to call its own until the 1980s. Prior to that it had used, first, the CP station, and then the attractive brick Canadian Northern station.)

From North Bay the line angled northwest, through the forests of the Canadian Shield, again drawing a string of sawmill towns to track-side. Here the line passed through Desaulniers, River Valley and Crerar, before meeting the tracks of the Canadian Northern's Toronto branch at Capreol, to this day an important railway town.

The Canadian Northern was quickly followed by yet another transcontinental route, that of the Grand Trunk Pacific, built largely by the government of Wilfred Laurier. But it soon become evident that Canada could not support three separate national delusions. The burdens of the first world war sent the two newcomers into bankruptcy and into the waiting arms of the newly legislated Canadian National Railways, which, saddled with lines which were redundant and others it claimed were merely "uneconomical", began to dismantle much of its railway network. CN's rail line abandonments accelerated through the 1980s and 90s, until today few of Ontario's CN railway lines remain.

The line between Pembroke and Capreol, and through Algonquin Park, was among the latest to go. Abandoned in 1996, much of the right of way, at this writing, still awaits disposition. Proponents of the Trans Canada Trail are advocating the incorporation of the route into Canada's newest national "dream". Algonquin Park authorities, however, have not yet committed to that idea, leaving open the dreaded option that the route through the park might become yet another logging road.

 All Aboard -

The starting point for this route is in Pembroke. Despite its relatively remote locale, Pembroke could once claim three railway stations. The first was that of the Canadian Pacific, a magnificent stone structure, demolished by CP in the early 1980s. The second was erected by the Grand Trunk on a branch line which ran off of John Booth's railway near Golden. Known as the Pembroke and Southern, it was a short route with only three other stations on it. Nevertheless, the GT building was a surprisingly large masonry building with a squared tower at one corner. It stood at the corner of MacKay and Pembroke Sts, the site today of a small mall. The third station was that of the Canadian Northern at the south end of town, where its tracks crossed those of the GT, a location still called Pembroke Junction. It was replaced during the 1950s by a more modern flat-roofed station.

Today, Pembroke is the end of rail for CN's Canadian Northern line, while the PS line was removed in 1961. Trains of a new short line, Railtex, still rumble through on CP's historic western main line.

Sadly, Pembroke offers the railway enthusiast little in the way of historic landscapes or trackside vestiges. To make matters worse, the proliferation of malls around the city has turned downtown Pembroke

Grand Trunk Station, Pembroke, Ont.

This postcard shows downtown Pembroke's handsome GT station which has gone, in its place a minimall has been constructed.

into a shadow of its former self. In an effort to restore some interest in the old core, several murals depicting the city's history have been painted on the sides of the main buildings.

While the abandoned route leads west, and enters Algonquin Park along the banks of Indian Creek, the right of way has not yet been opened as a trail. The best means to follow the roadbed at this point, therefore, remains by car. It will be impossible to complete in a single day, however, as the distances along the gravel roads which stab into the park are considerable. Instead, take a tent and a canoe, and turn this chase into a holiday.

Follow Pembroke St west from the downtown through the suburban sprawl of what was formerly Stafford Township to Achray Road and turn west. At a T-intersection with CR 26, turn left, cross Highway 17, and then turn right onto CR 28. This becomes the Barren Canyon Road and leads you deep into Algonquin Park to the former CNo station sites of Achray and Agnone.

At 20.3 km (14 miles) past the park entrance watch for the signs to the Barren Canyon hiking trail. This striking chasm is one of the deepest gorges in Ontario, and little known beyond park users. At 31.6 km (20 miles) you may be able to make out the remains of a former log-

The station and other railway buildings at Achray in Algonquin Park.

ging camp. When you reach the turnoff to Achray campground, a short distance further along, follow that road to the shores of Grand Lake. Here, by the parking lot, you will see the freshly abandoned right of way. Near it are a pair of early structures, one a stone park office built in 1933, the other the fire ranger's cabin once occupied by painter Tom Thomson. The lake side cliff where he painted his famous "Jack Pine" is along the abandoned railway line beyond the eastern parking area. No railway structures have survived here.

Return to the Barren Canyon Road and continue for another 30 km (20 miles) to where the road bends sharply right and proceed to the North Travers Creek parking area. This site marks the location of the Pembroke Shook Mills which operated between 1929 and 1954. The railway point was known as Stuarts Spur, a short spur line which led to the mill.

Two km beyond the entrance to the parking lot, a 1 ½ km trail leads north to the site of the Pembroke Lumber Company's logging operation, a relatively recent operation that ran from the 1930s until it closed in 1977. After about another two km the dishes of the Institute for Space Terrestrial Science observatory come into view, although they are off limits to the public. Lake Travers, for a number of years, had a post office and a population numbering about three dozen.

Just beyond the observatory lies another testimony to the Ontario government's neglect of its own heritage. In 1933 the family of J.R.

The old store in Brent no longer serves train crews as it once did. Now it outfits canoers embarking upon the waters of the northern portion of the Park.

Booth built a lodge of logs. Because the structure resembled a turtle, it was known as the Turtle Club. Purchased by the government in 1973, this piece of park history was then demolished.

Until such time as a trail is opened on the road bed, the only way to reach the next feature, the village of Brent, is by road (unless you're canoeing downstream and care to challenge the difficult rapids of the Petawawa River). Return all the way back out to Highway 17, and follow it north to Deux Rivieres. Although it is a long journey, the route leads through the forests and the mountains which line the Ottawa River. About three km (two miles) past Deux Riviere, you turn onto the Brent Road for a jolting 40 km journey over a dirt road to the remote community of Brent.

Brent's history within the park is unique. It is the only town within the park to become a railway divisional point. Here the railway located a bunkhouse and restaurant for crews coming off their shift. The Brent Lumber Company operated here from 1921–31, providing the railway with its only local source of revenue. The community consisted of the station, the store, and several dozen cabins which line the dirt streets.

When passenger service ended in 1960, the residents found they

The sawmill village of Kiosk stood until the early 1980s when MNR ordered everyone out. The ministry's new "wilderness" plan for Algonquin Park allowed no room for industries or villages.

had no way out in the winter. MNR refused to plough the road, and the townspeople were forced to move out. Today, the little station, boarding house and other railway-owned buildings have gone. The old store remains, however, now outfitting canoeists, while several of the former railway houses are used as summer cottages.

Part way along the road is a plaque describing the Brent meteor crater. However, it is now filled with water and surrounded by trees, so that the only way to distinguish its circular features is from the air.

To reach the site of Kiosk, the next town on the line, you must once again return to Highway 17, and follow it to Mattawa. Rail enthusiasts should pause here, however, and board the Timber Train. A new tourist attraction, the refurbished coaches follow the CPR's old "Moccasin Line" along the Quebec side of the river to the planned mill town of Temiscamingue. The all-day trip passes forested mountains, and occasionally soars above deep gorges to sweeping views across the river.

Travel west from Mattawa (which has some small modern motels) for 19 km(12 miles) to Highway 630 and follow it 29 km (20 miles) to Kiosk. Sadly, nothing but rubble and old paths remain of the townsite. However, you will find a campground, and access to the less crowded canoe routes of the northern park. In fact, interrupted by only a few

Kiosk's simple station typified the style of most of the CNo's stations located within the Park.

portages, you can follow the route of the railway by canoe through Kioshkokwi, Mink, Chiacoan, and Cedar lakes to Brent and the start of the Petawawa River.

Before visiting North Bay, you may want to make your way to the vanished village of Fossmill, and the one-time station village of Alderdale. To reach these locations, follow Highway 64 south of Highway 17 to Highway 11 which leads to Powassan. From Powassan drive east on Memorial Park Dr for 10 km (6.5 miles) to Alderdale Rd and turn right to enter Alderdale. It survives as a residential hamlet, although its orientation beside the abandoned right of way, and the vacant station grounds, confirm its former reliance upon the railway. In fact, many local landowners, in anticipation of a possible divisional point, speculated in lands, only to learn to their impoverishment that the railway had no such plans.

From Alderdale drive south to the next corner, Chiswick Line, and turn left and then right onto Bellcairn Rd. Continue on to Pioneer Rd and turn left. Look in a farm yard on the north side of the road to see the relocated Alderdale station, a simple red wooden structure that typified many of the modest stations along this portion of the line. Turn right onto Maple Rd and then left onto Fossmill Rd. Here you will pass through the community of Wasing which also had a small station on the railway line. Continue east for another 6 km to the end of the road. Here you can walk along the old right of way a short distance to the overgrown site of Fossmill. Although, other than a bit of rubble and weeds, little remains to see.

When you enter North Bay via Highway 11 and 17, you pass the new ONR train and bus station at the crossing on the east. To reach North Bay's two historic stations, follow Fisher St to Oak St where the wonderful old stone CP station sits at the west end of Ferguson. The former Canadian Northern station, now boarded and vandalized, and likely doomed unless a savior comes soon, sits east along Fraser near Second St. Brick and stone, it is two stories at the road entrance.

Spend some time in North Bay. A new park now stretches along the waterfront of Lake Nipissing where you can cruise the lake on the *Chief Commanda.* You can board the *Northlander* (it was still running early in 2000) north to Cochrane to catch the *Polar Bear Express* to Moosonee, or voyage south to Muskoka or Toronto.

Meanwhile, the abandoned right of way makes its way northwesterly through town, paralleling Main St back out to the junction of Highway 17. From here you follow 17 west to Sturgeon Falls where you take Highway 64 north to Field. Up until the 1990s the town's only two historic buildings were the two-storey train station and the massive computerized saw mill. Sadly, neither building was saved, and the town today has little to offer either the historian or the rail buff.

In Field, cross the bridge over the river and turn left onto highway 539. This route takes you through some rugged landscape of farms and forests, and past the railside sawmill villages of Desaulniers, where the main street that led to track is now empty of buildings, River Valley, and Azen. Keep in mind that beyond River Valley the road has no exit, and so at this point you would have to follow Highway 539 south to Warren, back on Highway 17.

While it is possible to drive into the ghost town of Crerar, the road is seasonal and not passable year round. To reach it, turn north at Markstay from Highway 17 and travel 10 km to the end of the maintained road, and then continue for another 6 km to Lake Ashigami. The station and railway village lay along the right of way, while the sawmill and mill worker's village stood beside the lake.

Built in the style of early stations, the VIA station at Capreol was designed and constructed during the late 1980s and opens daily to welcome the "Canadian."

The last stop on this journey is Capreol, a still bustling railway town north of Sudbury. To reach it turn north from Highway 17 onto Regional Road 90 at Coniston. At Garson turn right onto RR 86 which leads into Skead, another trackside mill town, but one from a later era. The mill has gone, but the solid homes still stand.

But to reach Capreol, you need to turn north from RR 86 onto RR 85. Capreol is where you encounter the Toronto branch of the Canadian Northern, today CN's busy main line to the west. A new passenger station, tastefully designed to resemble an old style railway station, still opens each day when the world's most beautiful train, VIA Rail's "Canadian", comes to call.

RR 80 leads south from Capreol into Sudbury where you can see another historic station, that of the CPR, on Elgin St (that railway company's busy yards sprawl beside it). Although Sudbury's history began with the railway, then known as Sudbury Junction, it boomed with the discovery of copper and then, more importantly, nickel. The Big Nickel tourist attraction, located at the junction of Lorne St and Big Nickel Road, explains the history of the mines, and offers a view of the Copper Cliff refinery, with the world's tallest stack. Here too is a tribute to the reforestation of the sulphur-blackened moonscape that once plagued this interesting town.

24.

The Three "Nip's", The Nip and Tuck, the Nipissing Central and the Nipigon Tramway: Bruce Mines, Cobalt and Nipigon

For most residents of Ontario's northland, dependency upon rail travel remains a recent memory. Some rail lines, however, are so enshrouded in the "mists of time," that few locals can even recall them. Such is the case of the three "Nip's".

The Nip and Tuck, or, the Bruce Mines and Algoma Railway

Of the three, the most colourful was the Nip and Tuck. This of course was not its original name. Rather it was given to the railway by doubtful local residents who saw in its rocky and barren route little hope for any success.

The line actually went by a few names. The first, in 1898, was the Bruce Copper Mines. This company operated a large stamp mill and coal dock in the village of Bruce Mines, connected by a mile of railway. A year later, another copper mine opened, this one on the shores of Rock Lake about 22 km (15 miles) north of Bruce Mines. Here were a large mill, a station and a small townsite, all located about two miles from the mine. To ship out the mineral, the company incorporated a railway and named it the Bruce Mines and Algoma Railway. Its southern terminus was two miles north of Bruce Mines on the CPR's Algoma branch, a route which had been put through from Sudbury to Sault Ste Marie about 15 years earlier.

But a terminus that halted such a short distance shy of the lake made little sense, and in 1903, the BMA was extended to the shore, where it established a junction with the BCM. With two large mines on its route the success of BMA seemed assured. But that would not be the case. The Bruce Copper Mines shipped very little by rail, and then in 1903 the Rock Lake mine closed. This left the BMA to haul a few

The main street of Bruce Mines still reflects its boom town roots.

farm and forestry products south, and coal from its coal dock north to the CPR.

By 1904 it had lost over $5,000. But closing the line wasn't in the cards, at least not yet. In 1904 the BMA got the unimaginable: permission to build north, not just to connections with the transcontinental routes of the C.P., the Canadian Northern, and the as-yet-to-be-built National Transcontinental, but all the way to James Bay!

Although some surveying was done, when the line's only two engines collided head-on, killing one crew member, its expansion plans collapsed. From 1905 to 1912, it was officially listed as "inactive," but not yet abandoned. Then, unexpectedly, things began to look up. Near the town of Bruce Mines a new rock quarry opened, the only access to which was along the old BCM, which, happily, the BMA just happened to own.

Full of hope, it bought three new engines and gave itself a new name, the Lake Huron and Northern Ontario Railway. Shortly after, another large customer came on board, the Mond Nickel Company, which owned a smelter at Victoria Mines, far to the east, now a ghost town. But Mond wasn't interested in copper. Rather, it was after the more common quartz to be used as a furnace flux.

Soon trains were rolling back up to Rock Lake, although the road bed was uneven, and the bridges so rickety that train crews would not remain on board while the engines crossed them. Instead, the fireman would cross a bridge ahead of the train, while the engineer tied the throttle to a low speed, and disembarked. When the creaking crew-less engine finally made it to the other side of the bridge, the fireman would climb back on and halt the train to await the engineer.

It was a sign of things to come. Profits did not materialize as hoped and in 1917 amounted to a mere $1,600. To pay off the mortgage, however, a profit of $35,000 was needed Then, in 1921, when the Mond closed, so did the Nip and Tuck. Rail remained in place until the 1930s, after which the right of way was sold to adjacent owners. Today, little trace remains.

 All Aboard --

Your route starts in the historic town of Bruce Mines, situated on Highway 17, and the oldest on Lake Huron's north shore. Follow the road from the Bruce Mines Museum south to Jacks Island where some remains of the coal dock can still be seen. The Bruce Mines station, and its junction with the BCM, stood a little east of today's Highway 581, about one block north of Highway 17.

Follow 581 north from Highway 17 until you reach the CPR crossing, and the village of Bruce Station which grew up by the tracks. The station was removed in the late 1970s, however, a few older buildings which once served the needs of the railway still stand. The Nip and Tuck right of way, although scarcely discernible, can be determined by a row of vegetation east of the crossing.

Continue north on 581 to the hamlet of Rydal Bank. On the way, the old right of way lies to the west of the highway, indiscernible from the ground. At Rydal Bank, the right of way crossed to the east of the highway, and then back west where a lane now occupies the roadbed. Here the road bed swung west to follow the south bank of the Thessalon River, and the south shore of Ottertail Lake.

To follow it, turn left from 581 at Rydal Bank. After a short distance the road occupies the road bed itself. After passing the lake, keep left at the Y intersection, and, after about 5 km, take the first road to the right.

This leads north to Plummer, by the bridge over the Thessalon River where McCarty Station stood a short distance east. Here, where the road hugs the shore of Gordon Lake, it once more occupies the old right of way for a short distance, before the right of way angles west. After paralleling the road for about 3 km, it swings east across the road to follow the bank of a small creek on the north side of the bridge. It is next to indiscernible however.

At the foot of a steep cliff, where the creek enters Rock Lake, some of the road bed has survived. From the intersection with Highway 683, turn right to the first lane on the right and follow it for a short distance to the lake shore. This leads to the small settlement of Rock Lake, the home of the mine and mill workers, and the end of the line, although the tracks continued east to the mill.

The Nipissing Central

One of northern Ontario's most colourful boom and bust areas is that around Cobalt. Following the discovery of silver in 1903, the town of Cobalt was thrown together where no town should have gone. Here were steep ridges of hard rock, separated by narrow crevices. Soon wooden houses crowned those rock tops at nearly every angle while roads were left to make their way among the outcrops. The building of the Temiskaming and Northern Ontario railway guaranteed the silver a route out, and Cobalt boomed to a population of nearly 10,000. More than 52 mines clanged into the hard rocky hillsides.

With the growth in the number of mining camps, it was felt that the booming area needed an electric railway line to provide more effective local service. One of the most critical reasons was that because Cobalt occupied a number of mining claims, no alcohol was allowed, and the nearest watering hole was in Haileybury. Thus, when the cars began operating in 1910, they were packed with thirsty miners headed for the Vendome Hotel, the route's first terminus.

Then in 1911, the NC was bought out by the TNO, not so much for the route, but rather to obtain its federal charter, which the provincially chartered TNO lacked, and which they needed to extend their tracks into Quebec. In 1912 the NC was extended into New Liskeard with a new terminal at the Wabi river, and branches to mines at Kerr Lake, and the Crown Reserve.

Its route took it from Argentite St in Cobalt, along a ravine north of Lang St and behind a residential area. It then followed a private right of way until it approached North Cobalt where it crossed the TNO on high concrete abutments. Its car barns were located in North Cobalt, at the halfway point of its route. From the barns the route went east on Lakeview Rd to Main St, now Carter Blvd, to the end of the street where it angled northeasterly to Georgina Rd and along that route into Haileybury via Blackwell and Ferguson Aves. The Vendome stood at the corner of Ferguson and Browning.

From Haileybury it continued along today's Lakeshore Rd and into downtown New Liskeard. The Kerr Lake branch was a four-mile link to the several silver mines operating in the hills south and east of the town. At the end of the line were a yard, small station and office building.

But like most interurbans, the NC was short-lived. In 1917 a fire in the car barns destroyed most of the rolling stock. The Kerr Lake branch was closed in 1925, and then in 1927, the Ferguson Highway was opened connecting Timmins and Toronto. When the new high-way was paved in 1935 the buses began to arrive and the NC ended its service, although some rail remained in place until the 1960s.

 **All Aboard** -

Not too surprisingly, there remains little to see. To follow the route, take Highway 11B out of Cobalt towards Haileybury. Between Cobalt and North Cobalt, the right of way can be discerned west of the ONR, and in a couple of places is occupied by private driveways. Near the southern edge of North Cobalt, the concrete abutments which carried the NC over the TNO are visible beside the highway.

In North Cobalt you will find the NC's only surviving structure, the large car barns which still stand on Lakeview Dr just west of 11B. The route from there into Haileybury and to New Liskeard has been oblit-erated by road widening and paving.

Cobalt is one of Ontario's most fascinating areas to explore, ghost railways or not. The TNO station in Cobalt, custom designed during

Top: North of Cobalt, the cars of the Nipissing Central crossed the tracks of its parent company, the TNO.

Left: The NC car barns are the only surviving structures from the line.

An old NC coach lives out its last days as a storage shed in North Cobalt.

its heyday, has been restored as a private museum. The few boomtown buildings that haven't been demolished or burned are a reminder of a lusty era when boom towns sprang up overnight, and looked it.

A self-guiding driving tour takes you through the silver fields south of the town where skeletal headframes appear above a young forest, and Roman-like ruins remain from the mills and mineshafts.

South of North Cobalt, down the picturesque Lorrain Valley, lurk the ruins of the ghost town of Silver Centre. Once home to 700 residents, only rubble remains, strewn through the bush. A branch line from the TNO once led here to a boxy two-storey wooden station of the type which the TNO built wherever it needed more room to accommodate its agents.

Cobalt is an area of ghosts. The old Nipissing Central is just one of those spectres.

The Nipigon Tramway

If the first two "Nip's" are faded memories, the Nipigon Tramway is nearly gone and forgotten. In 1912 the federal government of Wilfred Laurier was busy building yet another transcontinental railway. While the Grand Trunk was building the western section, named the Grand

A view along the Nipigon River where barges hauled flat cars to be pulled along the Nipigon Tramway.

Trunk Pacific, the government was responsible for the eastern portion, a line known as the National Transcontinental. Because the Canadian Pacific and the Canadian Northern had already laid claim to the route south of Lake Nipigon and along the Superior shore, the NT opted for a route which passed to the north of Lake Nipigon.

Getting construction material to this remote area, however, proved a burdensome hurdle. From several locations on the CPR, horses hauled wagons loaded with material along narrow and jolting tote roads, a time consuming process. One of the easiest routes was a water route which followed the Nipigon River and Lake Nipigon.

At the town of Nipigon, the contractors built a wharf on the river, just upstream from Lake Superior and beneath the CPR's high level bridge. At this point supplies were loaded onto narrow gage flatcars situated on barges. The barges were floated 18 km (12 miles) across Helen Lake and up the Nipigon River to Alexander Landing. However, a number of rapids on the Nipigon River proved to be an impossible obstacle, and the Nipigon Tramway was built to bypass them.

Twenty-five km (16 miles) long, this narrow gauge railway was oper- ated by the Nipigon Construction Company. At Alexander Point, the flat cars were offloaded and hooked up behind a saddle tank engine for the 18-mile journey to South Bay on Lake Nipigon. Following a 110 km (70-mile) trip across the lake and into Ombabika Bay, the flat cars were once more connected to the donkey engines for the final 15 km (10 miles) to Ferland, its connection on the National Transcontinental Railway.

With the completion of the NTR, the Nipigon Tramway became redundant and was abandoned. As recently as 1972, some government maps were still showing the route as an "abandoned railway" although portions are now used by snowmobilers and to access summer camp sites.

You will find the right of way on Highway 585 about 12 km (8 miles) north of Nipigon near the Cameron Falls power dam.

25.

The Smoky Line, the Spruce Falls Power and Paper Company Railway: Kapuskasing to Smoky Falls

The Smoky Line is about as remote as a ghost railway is going to get. And cold. It is here in Kapuskasing that General Motors tested their prototype automobiles for cold weather durability. It is here, too, that in 1912 the National Transcontinental Railway extended it trackage to the Kapuskasing River and named their station McPherson.

During the first world war the site served as a prisoner of war camp. Who, after all, would want to escape from food and warmth into bone-numbing cold or clouds of black flies? Following the war to end all wars, the government tried to open northern Ontario. Their propaganda touted the land as rich and fertile, capable of supporting crops and livestock. It did not, however, prove capable of supporting people.

Although many were drawn by the photos and descriptions, most were out-of-work soldiers, or impoverished city dwellers (homelessness is not unique to modern Ontario). Once here they were quickly defeated by the flies, the isolation, and the soil which was hard when dry, and gumbo when wet. Ontario's "new north" quickly became a ghost colony.

But it would not long remain that way. Pulp companies began to eye the vast supply of pulp wood and the ready availability of water power for potential hydro sites. The Kapuskasing and Mattagami River watersheds had both. In 1922 the Spruce Falls Pulp and Paper Company chose the banks of the Kapuskasing River for their new mill, and a planned town, Kapuskasing. Power from Sturgeon Falls was close at hand, and the tracks of what had become the CNR allowed shipment east to Montreal or south to Toronto via the TNO.

About 80 km (50 miles) north another series of falls tumbled over

A narrow gauge logging train, similar to those which travelled on the Smoky Line, is on display in Atikokan Ontario.

the Mattagami River. These were the Smoky Falls. In 1926, the Spruce Falls Power and Paper Company Railway, or the Smoky Line, was opened to the falls where two townsites were established. At Little Long Rapids there stood a construction camp for the building of a series of hydro dams, while the Smoky Falls community stood a bit further north.

In 1945 a branch line was extended to Neshin Lake to haul out lumber from the Opasatika River area. At Neshin Lake, wood was floated in on the Opasatika River for shipment to the Bennet Lake cut yard where logs were chopped into millable lengths.

The railway was a single purpose line—to tap the remote reaches of flat forest north of Kapuskasing. Stations were located at Neshin Junction, Lake Bennet, Smoky Falls, and Kapuskasing

Smoky Falls is the older and more northerly of the two townsites. Although it did not register a population with the census takers in 1941, it contained 95 residents a decade later. And that's about as large as it got, falling to 45 in 1961, and holding at 53 in 1971. Little Long Rapids townsite had one purpose only and that was to house workers for the construction of a series of hydro dams. Nearly 600 people resided there between 1961 and 1966, according to the census.

One of the last VIA Rail trains to call at Kapuskasing sits in front of the handsome brick station. Service was eliminated by the Mulroney government in 1990.

Transportation was on a mixed train known as the Little Long Express. Despite the nickname, travel was slow, especially in spring when frost heaved the tracks into a mild roller coaster. Otherwise, transportation on the Smoky Line consisted of specially outfitted railbuses and even a 1963 Plymouth station wagon.

By 1975, the limits were nearing depletion, and trucks began hauling logs into Kap. Tracks were lifted and most residents moved away. Despite its remoteness, much of the old roadbed is accessible by passenger car, and in places now forms the roads themselves.

 ## All Aboard

This trip starts at the government building on the west end of Kapuskasing on Highway 11. Here, on the west side of the bridge that crosses the river, you can yet see some rail embedded in the asphalt. You won't see the station, however, which stood on the north side, for the buildings and yards have been removed. Look behind the government building, however, to see some the "speeders" which once navigated the line.

From Kapuskasing to Ghost Creek, the line, with many of its bridges burned, is navigable only by snowmobiles. You can, however, reach the more northerly sections of the line by car by taking the Pearce Hall Road north from Highway 11 a short distance east of Kapuskasing. It is one of those northern phenomena, a private road with public access, in other words, a logging road. It is, however, wide enough for passenger vehicles, although you should drive it only during the dry season.

After about 40 km (25 miles) you will reach the old railway roadbed. If you follow the roadbed a short distance southwest, you come upon a row of rail passenger cars, used until recently by the Spruce Falls company as guest accommodation for fishermen to the area.

While the railway roadbed continues to the northeast, several of the bridges are out here as well, and the route is not navigable. Instead, continue north on the forest road to a Y intersection. The fork which leads east is the main travelled portion, and takes you back to the right of way. The clearings which you see here were the site of the Bennett cut yard. From this point north to Smoky Falls, the road bed has been "upgraded" and although only a single lane, can take most passenger cars although no buildings have survived.

For the next 22 km (14 miles) the route is straight, the terrain depressingly flat, while the hydro line beside you reveals what the line was really for. At the first of the large dams, you will find the clearings for the vacated construction camp of Little Long Rapids. About 8 km (5 miles) further along the road, the right of way ends at the ghost town of Smoky Falls. Here you will see about a half dozen houses, the one-time school and large staff house. You will also see more of the dams which draw electricity from this once turbulent river.

To return, you must go back the way you came in. Alternatively, from the Little Long Rapids a road leads east to the ONR trackside community of Fraserdale. The distance is less, about 45 km (28 miles), and you end up at Highway 807 which leads you south to the town of Smooth Rock Falls, another pulp mill town, and also on Highway 11. Here you will find yourself about an hour's drive east of Kapuskasing, and a like distance west of Cochrane.

Although it is not a popular tourist route, Ontario's northeast has much to offer. From Cochrane, with its unusually wide main street,

Kapuskasing is an unusual town for Ontario's far north, having been laid out as a planned town by a firm of New York planners in 1923.

you can ride the popular Polar Bear Express, the summer excursion train to Arctic tidewater and the Cree community of Moosonee. On an island in the Moose River, Moose Factory is one of Ontario's oldest permanent settlements.

Kapuskasing has some startling sights of its own. While most northern towns were laid out in a grid network of streets, Kapuskasing was a planned town. Here the main street forms a circle in the town centre, while from the river, and the town's main public buildings, the roads radiate outward like a fan. The architecture is out of place as well, displaying tudoresque styles more common in the south.

The town's two most historic buildings are the old Kapuskasing Inn, and the handsome former CN railway station where a steam engine and string of vintage railway coaches make up the local museum. If you want more information on the Smoky Line, it's the place to get it.

26.

The Thunder Bay Nipigon and St Joe Railway, A Phantom Railway: Thunder Bay to Armstrong

Many of Ontario's early railway builders harboured "pie in the sky" plans of how grand their schemes would be. The Brockville Westport and Sault Ste Marie Railway, for example, failed to reach beyond Westport. The James Bay Junction remained little more than a spur line until the Canadian Northern incorporated it into their national route. Even then, it never came close to James Bay.

But the grandly named Thunder Bay Nipigon and St Joe Railway never even made it off the map.

The turn of the century was the heady railway building era for northwestern Ontario. The Canadian Pacific had inaugurated its first national trains only 15 years earlier, the Canadian Northern was busy surveying its national route along the shores of Lakes Nipigon and Superior, while the Port Arthur Duluth and Western was making it way to the iron ranges of Minnesota where a proposed link with Duluth never materialized, (please see *Ghost Railways of Ontario: Volume One*). And in Ottawa talk raged over where yet another national line, Prime Minister Wilfred Laurier's National Transcontinental Railway line, would be built.

Furthermore, promoters of New Ontario, as the area was called, saw gold in every glitter, and farmland in every pine stand, if only a railway was there to open it all up.

It was into this wonderland that the Thunder Bay Nipigon and St Joe Railway was first promoted. In fact, the words on the cover of its prospectus could barely contain the optimism: "Farms! Homes!", it screamed, "Farming lands, grazing lands, dairy lands, sheep lands, spruce lands, gold, silver, iron, copper, limestone and marble." It was Shangri-La. And it was all north of Lake Superior.

The line was proposed to run from Thunder Bay (Port Arthur, as it was then called) north for 130 km (80 miles) to Dog Lake and Lake Nipigon, then northwest for another 175 km (110 miles) to Lake St Joseph.

Along the way the mineral deposits were said to include an "enormous deposit" of slate iron shale, an "immense" deposit of marble, "the largest of the kind in the world," and at Lake St . Joseph itself, lignite coal beds. Between Thunder Bay and Lake Nipigon were said to lay two million acres of "arable" land, which "equals that of the famous Rainy River valley." Here dairy cattle would graze lazily, supplying creameries with great quantities of milk. Trains would carry out the milk and bring in fresh fish. "The crowning beauty of this section is in its farming lands," the prospectus concluded.

Tourists, it touted, would rush to see the Dog Lake Falls with a drop "twice the height of Niagara," as well as a wall of white quartz, known as the "Chinese Wall," 30 m or 80 feet wide and 17 m or 50 feet high, and "one of the curiosities of America." The "summer tourists, fishing campers, clubbers and cottagers" would pump more than a million dollars into the economy of Ontario, the promoters claimed

It's too bad that nobody believed them. Despite their heady optimism, the railway was never built. The completion of the Canadian Northern, and the start of the government-sponsored National Transcontinental, sank the TNJ into the well of wishful thinking. Now, the very regions which would have been tapped by the doomed line were made accessible by the two new transcontinental lines.

Even the resource riches failed to materialize. And few settlers arrived other than gold seekers, cottagers and hunters, and pulp companies. Some small gold deposits were discovered on the shores of Sturgeon Lake, but the mines were short-lived and more easily accessed by the National Transcontinental Railway from Savant Lake. No coal deposits were ever mined, no ore extracted, and even the mysterious "Chinese Wall" was never heard of again.

 All Aboard -

Today, the line has been forgotten, the prospectus gathering dust in the archives. During the 1960s, extensive highway building opened

The harsh landscape north of Nipigon demonstrates the obstacles of terrain which the TNJ's builders would have had to overcome.

still more of the northwest, including a forest road from Thunder Bay to Armstrong. Now known as Highway 527, it generally follows the route of the proposed line through the very area which the railway would have tapped. It is a lonely road, 250 km (150 miles) long, passing through desolate area laid bare by clear-cut logging, and accessing only a few small First Nations villages.

At the northern end of the highway, Armstrong is a former divisional town for the National Transcontinental Railway. Houses, stores and hotels lined the vast yards behind the two-storey station. For several decades, a radar base sat at the eastern end of the settlement, guarding against hostile Soviet missiles. Now abandoned, its buildings are reused as homes, businesses, and the community's only motel. Meanwhile, the station sits vacant and vandalized. A strange sight every day is the arrival of VIA's luxury train, the *Canadian*, an anomaly in the midst of Armstrong's rugged northern simplicity.

Some farms were cleared between Nipigon and Thunder Bay, but nowhere near the vast area predicted by the railway promoters.

While northwestern Ontario remains a lonely yet lovely land, the bounties dreamed of by the promoters of Thunder Bay, Nipigon and St Joe Railway, remained just that, dreams.

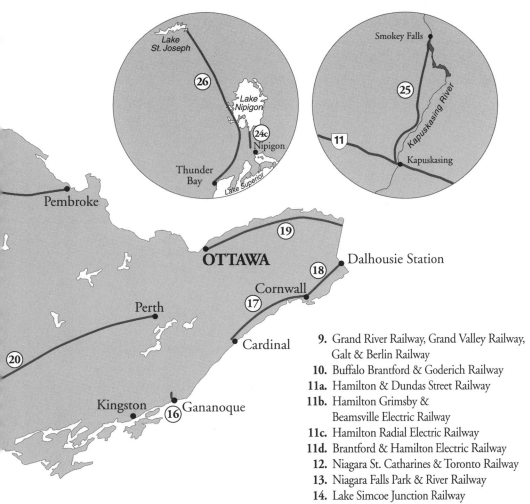

Legend

1a. Windsor Essex & Lakeshore Rapid Railway
1b. Woodstock, Thames Valley & Ingersoll Railway
1c. Chatham Wallaceburg & Lake Erie Railway
1d. London & Lake Erie Railway
2. Lake Erie & Detroit River Railway
3. Wellington Grey & Bruce Railway, Kincardine Branch
4. Stratford & Lake Huron Railway
5. St. Mary's & Western Railway
6. Toronto Grey & Bruce Railway
7. Lake Erie & Northern Railway
8. Toronto Hamilton & Buffalo Railway

9. Grand River Railway, Grand Valley Railway, Galt & Berlin Railway
10. Buffalo Brantford & Goderich Railway
11a. Hamilton & Dundas Street Railway
11b. Hamilton Grimsby & Beamsville Electric Railway
11c. Hamilton Radial Electric Railway
11d. Brantford & Hamilton Electric Railway
12. Niagara St. Catharines & Toronto Railway
13. Niagara Falls Park & River Railway
14. Lake Simcoe Junction Railway
15. Grand Trunk Railway (original)
16. Thousand Islands Railway
17. Grand Trunk Railway (original)
18. Glengarry & Stormont Railway
19. Canadian Pacific Railway (South Shore Line)
20. Ontario & Quebec Railway
21. Bracebridge & Trading Lake Railway
22. Huntsville & Lake of Bays Railway
23. Canadian Northern Railway
24a. Bruce Mines & Algoma Railway
24b. Nipissing Central Railway
24c. Nipigon Tramway
25. Spruce Falls Power & Paper Co. Railway
26. Thunder Bay Nipigon & St. Joseph Railway

Recommended Reading

Brown, Ron, *Ghost Railways of Ontario*, Polar Bear Press, Toronto, 1997.

Brown, Ron, *Ghost Towns of Ontario: A Field Guide, Volumes One and Two*, Polar Bear Press, Toronto 1997, 1999.

Bytown Railway Society, *Canadian Railway Station Guide*, Bruce Ballantyne ed., Ottawa Ont., 1998.

Cooper, J.I., "The Traction, The Story of the London and Lake Erie Railway," *Canadian Rail*, March 1968.

Currie, A.W. *The Grand Trunk Railway of Canada*, University of Toronto Press, 1957.

Dorman, Robert, *A Statutory History of Railways in Canada*, Canadian Institute of Guided Ground Transport, Kingston, 1987.

Due, John F., *The Intercity Electric Railway Industry of Canada*, University of Toronto Press, 1966.

Hardy, John R., *Rusty Rails, a photographic record of branchline railways in Midwestern Ontario, 1961-1996*, self published, Hanover, 1999.

Helm, Norman, *Tri-town Trolleys, the Story of the Nipissing Central Railway*, Highway Book Shop, Cobalt, 1984.

Hopkins, A.A., "An Ontario Short Line, The Smoky Line," *UCRS Newsletter*, 1964.

Jackson, John and John Burtniak, *Railways in the Niagara Peninsula*, Mika Press, Belleville Ontario, 1978.

Lloyd, Eric, "The Huntsville and Lake of Bays Railway," *Canadian Rail*, June 1982.

Long, Gary, "Phantom Train to Baysville; the Bracebridge and Trading Lake Railway," *The Muskoka Sun*, July 13, 1989.

Lombard, Jack, "Hiram Builds a Railway," *Canadian Rail*, Feb 1972.

MacKay, Donald, *The Peoples Railway, A History of Canadian National Railways*, Douglas and McIntyre, Vancouver, 1992.

Maclean, John A., "The Sunshine County Route, the Windsor Essex and Lake Shore Rapid Railway" *UCRS Newsletter*, Sept, 1982.

Maclean, John A., "Farewell to the T.H and B." *UCRS Newsletter*, May, 1981.

Merrilees, Andrew A., "Sixty Years Without Interurbans, The Dominion Power and Transmission Company in Hamilton," *UCRS Newsletter*, Sept, 1991.

"Make Room for the Seaway, Cornwall- Iroquois Track Relocation", *Railway Age*, Dec, 1957.

Mills, John M., *Cataract Traction, The Railways of Hamilton*, UCRS/Ontario Electric Railway Historical Association, 1971.

Mills, John M., *History of the Niagara St Catharines and Toronto Railway*, UCRS/Ontario Electric Railway Historical Association, 1967.

Mills, John M., *Traction on the Grand*, Railfare, 1977.

Rhodes, John, *Come Walking and Leave Early, A History of the Chatham, Wallaceburg and Lake Erie Railway*, self published, Chatham, 1982.

Rhodes, John, *Rails to the Heartland, A Pictorial History of Kent's Railways*, self published, Chatham, 1991.

Smith, Douglas N.W., *By Rail Road and Water to Gananoque*, Trackside Canada, 1996.

Todd, J. "The Nipigon Tramway," *Canadian Rail*, Oct, 1977.

Walker, Dr. Frank N., "Buffalo Brantford and Goderich Railway," *UCRS Newsletter*, January, 1954.

Watson, Peter, *The Great Gorge Route, P. Watson and Assoc*, Niagara Falls, 1997.

Wilson, Dale, "The Nip and Tick," *Canadian Rail*, Dec. 1976.

Wilson, Donald M., *The Ontario and Quebec Railway*, Mika Publishing, Belleville, 1984.

Index

Photo credits

p. 36   Canadian Inventory of Historic Buildings (CIHB), Parks Canada
p. 46   CIHB
p. 61   Len Appleyard Collection
p. 75   National Archives of Canada (PA 149457)
p. 90   Metropolitan Toronto Reference Library
p. 91   CIHB
p. 103   Len Appleyard Collection
p. 109   CN Archives
p. 144   United Counties Museum
p. 156   National Archives of Canada (PA 8676)
p. 158   CIHB (06-4-139)
p. 164   CP Archives (A-19949)
p. 175   CIHB (06144-1-4)
p. 178   Ontario Archives
p. 180   Ministry of Natural Resources
p. 188   CIHB
p. 191   Ministry of Natural Resources
p. 200   Ontario Archives

All other photos by Ron Brown